AT THE ALTAR OF SPEED

AT THE ALTAR

SPEED

The Fast Life and Tragic Death of Dale Earnhardt

LEIGH MONTVILLE

BROADWAY BOOKS

New York

BROADWAY

First Broadway Books trade paperback edition published 2002

Based on the photo layout, the credits from the top of a page to the bottom are as follows: Page 1: 1) International Motorsports Hall of Fame; 2) International Motorsports Hall of Fame; 3) International Motorsports Hall of Fame. Page 2: 1) Heinz Kluetmeier/*Sports Illustrated*; 2) John Iacono/*Sports Illustrated*; 3) Tony Tomsic/*Sports Illustrated*. Page 3: 1) George Tiedemann/*Sports Illustrated*; 2) Tony Tomsic/*Sports Illustrated*; 3) Tony Tomsic/*Sports Illustrated*. Page 4: 1) George Tiedemann/*Sports Illustrated*; 2) George Tiedemann/*Sports Illustrated*; 3) Brian Spurlock; 4) Michael C. Hebert; 5) George Tiedemann/*Sports Illustrated*. Page 5: 1) George Tiedemann/*Sports Illustrated*; 2) George Tiedemann/*Sports Illustrated*; 3) George Tiedemann/*Sports Illustrated*; 4) George Tiedemann/*Sports Illustrated*. Page 6: 1) George Tiedemann/*Sports Illustrated*; 2) George Tiedemann/*Sports Illustrated*; 3) George Tiedemann/*Sports Illustrated*. Page 7: 1) George Tiedemann/*Sports Illustrated*; 2) David Bergman/*Sports Illustrated*; 3) George Tiedemann/*Sports Illustrated*; 4) Phelan Ebenhack/*Orlando Sentinel*; 5) Don Burk/*Florida Times-Union*. Page 8: 1) Robert Padgett/Reuters; 2) Daniel Lenz/*News Daily*; 3) Les Duggins/*Herald-Journal*; 4) George Tiedemann/*Sports Illustrated*.

Photoedited by George G. Washington

Cataloging-in-Publication Data is on file with the Library of Congress.

ISBN 0-7679-0992-5

10 9 8 7 6 5 4 3 2 1

For Samantha

ACKNOWLEDGMENTS

Most of the material in this book was gathered in the three months after Dale Earnhardt's death. People handle grief in different ways. To those people who wanted to talk . . . thank you very much. To those who wished to remain silent . . . your silence is quite understandable. Special thanks to Humpy Wheeler, the unofficial soul of NASCAR. Thanks also to Lars Anderson, George G. Washington, Jason Kaufman, Luke Dempsey, Esther Newberg, Paul Doyle, to my kids, Leigh Alan and Robin, and to Mary Ellen, who took the whole ride . . .

And thanks, of course, to Dale. He lived the life and captured the imagination of an entire country.

PSALM NO. 3

Blessed are the knuckleheads . . .
Blessed are the long-haired, the unruly, the disenfranchised . . .
Blessed are the dropouts, the screwups, the ne'er-do-wells . . .
Blessed are the nervous, living in trailer-park double-wides,
*   scratching and clawing, not answering the bill collector's call . . .*
Blessed are the cowboys on their Saturday nights . . .
Blessed are the rowdy . . .
Blessed are the flawed. . . .

Blessed are the pipe fitters, the ironworkers, the wheel alignment
*   specialists, the carpenters and dishwashers and paper-or-plastic*
*   supermarket captives of a time clock . . .*
Blessed are the farmers . . .
Blessed are the housepainters . . .
Blessed are the firemen and cops and U.S. Postal workers and the
*   career enlisted military men, hashmarks down their pressed*
*   sleeves . . .*
Blessed are the truck drivers, alone against the night . . .
Blessed are the work-on-commission salesmen, bounced from
*   another office without a sale . . .*
Blessed are the security guards . . .
Blessed are the fry-order cooks . . .
Blessed are the commuters, stuck in traffic . . .
Blessed are the third-base coaches, the utility infielders, the
*   ground crew working in the sun . . .*
Blessed are the character actors and the stuntmen and the lighting
*   crew . . .*
Blessed are the bass guitar players. . . .

Blessed are the unappreciated with rough hands, calluses built
     stronger every day, dirt deep under the fingernails, Skat soap
     and hot water needed every night . . .
Blessed are the unnoticed with tired feet that are stuffed inside
     steel-toed work boots and door-to-door wing tips . . .
Blessed are the uncounted with tired legs that are stuffed inside
     denim and uniform cotton . . .
Blessed are the uncomfortable with hungover heads that are stuffed
     under hard hats in the morning . . .
Blessed are the untouched with still-beating hearts that are
     covered by pocket protectors filled with ball-point pens. . . .

Blessed are the hastily married . . .
Blessed are the divorced . . .
Blessed are the stepfathers . . .
Blessed are the stepchildren . . .
Blessed are the stepchildren of the stepchildren. . . .

Blessed are the weak, who want to be strong . . .
Blessed are the poor, who want to be rich . . .
Blessed are the inarticulate, who want to speak. . . .

Blessed are the frustrated. . . .

Blessed are the restless. . . .

A window to the imagination stays open . . .
A racetrack on a sunny day . . .
A black car steams from the back, get out of the way, get out
     of the way, pushing through the shiny, multicolored obstacles
     in front . . .
Get out of the way. . . .

A great roar comes from the car, from the crowd, from deep within
  each and every thoracic cavity . . .
Get out of the way. . . .
The action comes past in a blur. . . .

Blessed are the knuckleheads, most of us, caught wherever we are
  caught, doing whatever we are doing, wishing, looking to get
  outside our lives and fly . . .
Blessed is Dale . . .
Dale Earnhardt, 1951–2001 . . .
He found the way.

—Leigh Montville
March 2001

PREFACE

There might have been a hole in the sun. That was how different every-thing felt after Dale Earnhardt died. The props for familiar fun were laid out in their familiar places on this little piece of the infield at the Talladega Superspeedway eight weeks later—the canvas and plastic lawn chairs in front of Terry Higgins's thirty-foot Pace Arrow motor home, the camping tents and the coolers behind—but the day seemed as hollow as the beer keg that had been unloaded with a *boiiiiiing* from the side door on Thurs-day night at the end of the seven-hour drive from Hixson, Tennessee.

What now? What?

"A keg holds 170 cups of beer," Terry Higgins said, because this is what he always said, what everybody said, trip after trip. "OK, do the math. There were ten guys in the motor home. Two of them don't drink. . . ."

"And I couldn't drink because I was driving," Steve Fox said.

"And Steve couldn't drink because he was driving," Higgins contin-ued. "So that's seven guys who were drinking. The keg held 170 cups of beer. Do the math. Seven hours. Seven guys. The keg was empty when we got here."

What now? What?

For ten straight years, the mathematics of beer consumption had been a running boast, a challenge, a fine countrified primal scream of April as the same cast of midlife characters attended the Talladega 500, the first of NASCAR's two annual Winston Cup visits to the Alabama track. *The keg is for the trip and then we have twenty-nine cases of beer and six bottles of liquor for the weekend! Including a fifth of Jack and a fifth of Crown Royal! Do the math! Two years ago we RAN OUT of beer! We're here to kick some serious ass! We're here to party, we're here to . . .* What? The beer, the fun, now had become almost an obli-gation. The ass-kicking was out of the question.

The three days at the track stretched across the calendar as if they were some mandatory appearance at some mandatory function. Be there. Do the business. Go home. There was a joyless form to everything, but certainly no direction. One step simply followed another.

"We didn't know what to do," Terry Higgins said. "Should we come? Not come?

"We came. We're here. And we still don't know what to do.

"None of us."

An army without a cause is no army at all.

"The ten guys in that motor home, nine are Dale Earnhardt fans," Higgins said. "Solid Dale Earnhardt fans. Total. The tenth guy, Jim Davis, he's a Jeff Gordon fan, but even he loved Dale Earnhardt. Look at him. He's wearing a Dale Earnhardt hat."

"I like Gordon," Jim Davis said from underneath his black baseball cap, "but I know who's the king. There's never been another one like him. There never will be another one."

Dale . . .

Dale . . .

Dale . . .

The unexpected events of February 18, 2001, when the forty-nine-year-old stock car legend, the seven-time Winston Cup champion, The Intimidator himself, crashed his familiar No. 3 black Goodwrench racing machine into the wall at over 180 miles per hour on the final lap on the final straightaway of the Daytona 500, virtually dead on impact, had caused tremors across the country that no one could have expected. Who'd have thought something like this could have such an effect? The furniture of countless everyday lives somehow had been rearranged. More than rearranged. Someone had removed the big living-room couch. Maybe the color television set, too.

Who'd have thought?

"I watched the race on television at the bar. I saw the crash," Higgins said. "I knew he was hurt, just the way he hit, but he'd been in a lot of crashes. He'd always walked away. I was here for the one at Talladega in '96. The one where he was upside down and someone drove right into him? That looked a lot worse than this one. . . . Then I got the call. I was driving my son home. A guy said, 'Dale's dead.' I couldn't believe it. I'm not ashamed to say I started crying. I'm not ashamed at all."

Higgins, forty-three, is the owner of Andy Capp's, a bar on Hixson Highway. He is an average-sized guy, pop-out belly, brown hair, country-western mustache, skin turned pink by the sun. He fell in love with Earnhardt "back at the end of the seventies, back before he even was driving Winston Cup, when he was running the Sportsman series." The attraction pretty much was instantaneous. There was something dangerous and fun about this newcomer to the scene, this longhaired young guy with another country-western mustache who looked as if he had just rolled out from underneath your family sedan and said "Hey, the shocks look good, but Ah'd think about balancin' them tires."

This new guy didn't seem to know the driving rules, didn't care. Hell's bells, he'd make room where there wasn't room, dinging and danging, sending other cars off into spins, flying through the carnage like the Road Runner outwitting a fleet of Wile E. Coyotes. He drafted just a little bit closer, planting the front end of his Chevrolet right against someone else's ass at 200 miles per hour, just waiting for the right moment to burst into clean air and fly. He rode high when necessary, out in the gray of the track, closer to the walls, fearless—that's the word—just fearless. He was a real-life duke, giving a good middle finger to any real-life hazard.

"He was Elvis Presley in a black suit," Higgins says. "That's the best way I can explain it. He brought to NASCAR what Elvis Presley brought to rock 'n' roll. There were no holds barred. He didn't ask for anything, but he didn't give away anything. No matter where he was on the racetrack, he was always working. You could see him, even if he was 34th, he was still racing. He just loved it. I read one time that 'he could see where the air was.' I always felt he did."

It turned out that hitching on with Earnhardt for the ride at the beginning was like starting out with Sinatra at a supper club in Hoboken. One season led into the next and the next and the championships kept coming and the pile of accomplishments grew higher and higher. The kid from underneath the family car became the middle-aged owner of Learjets and yachts, bulldozers and chicken farms, richer than anyone at the best country club in town. Famous. He met with Presidents and boardroom poobahs, scuba-dived and hunted strange animals, sang with famous singers, got a little heavier in the bottom and a little thinner on top, yet never lost the core of his spirit, the competitiveness, the aggressiveness. He was still going, the crusty son of a bitch, heading into his fiftieth birthday at the same speed and with the same fire he always had.

Higgins held on to all this success as if he had a string tied to a hot air balloon. All the midlife boys in the motor home did. Anyone who liked Dale Earnhardt did. Dale was a man who gave you the best of returns on your emotional investments. Root for Dale and you win when he wins. He won all the time.

The trips to races became Dale pilgrimages. There was Bristol, up in the Tennessee mountains, the half-mile short track. Who was better at close quarters than Dale? The cars spun around as if they were inside a noisy washing machine. Who came out of the washing machine, more often than not, with the brightest smile? There were trips to Talladega, the 2.66-mile jet-strip tri-oval with the wicked banked turns, the speeds so fast that NASCAR mandated restrictor plates to calm everbody down. Who hated restrictor plates the most, thought they limited an unlimited sport? Who, nevertheless, was known as "The King of Restrictor-Plate Racing," just a year ago in October coming from 18th place in the last four laps, slicing through the gerrymandered suspense to win at the wire? There were trips to Atlanta every November, where the Winston Cup champion was crowned. Who stood up there at the end, accepting that check, getting that smoky cigarette kiss from the Winston bathing beauty and holding the trophy over his head? Who? Seven times, brother. Count 'em.

Higgins's devotion multiplied through the years. He had a gold race car medallion with a No. 3 in the front cast specially by a jeweler. Higgins wore it every day, a tribute to his own patron saint. He lit his cigarettes with a No. 3 lighter. He kept out the glare with a pair of black No. 3 sunglasses, the familiar red-and-white numeral just above the bridge of his nose. He bought Dale Earnhardt sweatshirts and Dale Earnhardt T-shirts and collected Dale Earnhardt bubble-gum cards and die-cast cars and programs and photos and hats and more hats.

When the first motor home died and Higgins bought the Pace Arrow, he wasted no time and had the new vehicle detailed in black stripes and red and white, adding so many key words and copywritten logos that it looked as if it were part of Richard Childress Racing, Dale's race team. A golf cart received similar treatment. The ultimate tribute came when he bought a black Chevy Lumina and had it detailed to look exactly like Dale's race car with the fat No. 3's on the doors and "Goodwrench" across the hood and all of the other sponsor stickers on the sides.

Talk about fantasy! He was The Intimidator! He was Dale!

And then Dale died.

"I went back to the bar," Terry Higgins said. "I didn't know what to do, but I knew I should do something. Everyone was all upset."

"There was over fifty grown men in there, all of 'em howling like hound dogs," Steve Fox said. "Nobody cared what anybody else thought."

Higgins decided the best move was to park the Lumina in front of the bar. He parked the detailed motor home. He parked the golf cart. He painted a sign, "Honk Three Times For Dale," and placed it on the Lumina. The noise began. For the entire night—*honk, honk, honk*—the tributes arrived. Everybody honked. Then the flowers started to arrive. There were wildflowers. There were floral arrangements. There were bouquets. There were cards, messages, expressions of condolence. Schoolkids and old folks and goobers and businessmen and just about anyone you could imagine added to the pile. Terry Higgins's bar became a grief center for the area.

Across the country, similar impromptu memorials were being built, piece by piece, hand by shaking hand. People simply appeared at any place Dale Earnhardt might have visited, might have touched. There were crowds at his corporate headquarters, Dale Earnhardt Incorporated (DEI), in Mooresville, North Carolina. There were crowds at the Daytona International Speedway, where he died. Every speedway on the circuit reported people appearing, praying, leaving a message, a bouquet, a piece of memorabilia. There were crowds at Earnhardt's still-uncompleted vacation home in West Palm Beach, Florida. People felt they had to do something, anything, to let their sadness breathe.

"The television stations, the newspapers, came and did stories," Terry Higgins said. "I guess they were pretty good, the stories. I have a tape and people tell me it's good, but I haven't seen it. I just can't watch it. Not yet."

———————

The hope was that the Talladega weekend might bring answers, but it really didn't. The midlife boys from the Dale Earnhardt motor home from Hixson tried. They drank all but four beers from the twenty-nine cases, drank all the liquor, rode the Dale Earnhardt golf cart through the infield campers, offering Mardi Gras beads to young women to expose their physical endowments, chatted up the stock car neighbors, let the sounds and smells of the racing run through their bodies, but the old spirit of the old occasions was missing.

"It's just not the same," Terry Higgins said from behind his Dale Earnhardt sunglasses. "I don't think it'll ever be the same."

Should he root for Dale Earnhardt Jr., No. 8, the slender son, the kid, racing under the weight of all this sentiment? Should he root for Kevin Harvick, No. 29, the rookie who had replaced Earnhardt, the number changed and the car painted silver? Should he find someone new? Who would that be? How could that be? He never did find the answer. He rooted for no one.

"It's all so sad," Terry Higgins said in the Alabama sunshine, another cigarette and another beer in hand.

Some of the midlife boys were standing on top of the motor home, watching the action. Bobby Hamilton was on the way to winning the race, a calm and caution-free affair, mostly a motorized parade, everyone afraid of the speeds and the possible collisions, reminded of the danger in the drivers' meeting by Michael Waltrip, a driver for Earnhardt's team. There was no drama, no bite. There was no reason, really, for all of this. Sad.

A black flag with the No. 3 hung at half-mast from the antenna on the motor home. A hand-painted sign, "In Memory of THE INTIM-IDATOR, 1951 to 2001," was stretched across the windshield. A funeral wreath, left over from the tribute in Hixson, hung below the sign. The artificial flowers were pink and blue and white.

"You know how sad this made me?" Terry Higgins said. "See those boys on the roof? I love 'em all. One of 'em's my son. If one of those boys fell off right now, broke his neck and died, I wouldn't feel any worse than I do about Dale Earnhardt. And that's the honest-to-God truth."

Only one moment had made any sense at all, one moment in three days. On the third lap of the race, while the Fox televison crew went silent, as the cars came blowing past, noisy and proud, Terry Higgins and the midlife boys had raised their right hands and held up three fingers to the sky. A sea of right hands, over 150,000 right hands, had done the same thing.

No one was alone.

1

AT THE ALTAR

A man in Cocoa Beach, Florida, plowed a giant, 353-foot No. 3 in his pasture. He said he just wanted to do it. To honor Dale. . . .

A thirty-five-year-old tow truck operator in Kenosha, Wisconsin, finished work, picked up his son and his father, and started driving. Twenty hours later, they were in Mooresville in front of the offices of Dale Earnhardt Incorporated. Just wanted to be there. He said he had left money with friends back in Kenosha to rent a billboard to say goodbye to Dale. . . .

A traveler from Los Angeles reported on the Internet that he was near Daytona Beach, taking pictures of a Titan rocket launch from the Space Center a week after the accident. The contrails from the rocket, moved by the wind, formed a giant No. 3 in the sky. He posted a picture. . . .

The proprietor of Tropical Tattoos in Daytona Beach, Florida, said he did a number of Dale Earnhardt tattoos on a number of bodies. He said he did two on the Monday after the accident. . . .

Crowds gathered. People cried.

Everywhere you looked, if you looked hard enough, there seemed to be a tribute. Something. . . .

THE CRASH

The intelligent head argued with the intelligent eyes. That was the thing. The eyes saw the severity of the crash. The eyes had seen other crashes in other places, the same speed, the same angle, the same unmerciful thud against a concrete wall. The eyes knew something terrible had happened. The intelligent head knew Dale Earnhardt was involved. He would be all right.

Eyes vs. head. What was a television color commentator supposed to say?

"How about Dale?" Darrell Waltrip asked into his Fox Sports microphone late on that Sunday afternoon of February 18, 2001. "I hope he's OK."

"Of course he's OK," the head screamed in response. "That's Dale. He walks away. Dale Earnhardt. He always walks away."

"I just hope Dale's OK," Waltrip said again into his microphone. "I guess he's all right, isn't he?"

The emotions that crowded inside the broadcast booth at the Daytona International Speedway were too much, too much, way too much to handle. Jesus, Good Lord, they were. Look out the window at one spot on the track and there was the surprise winner of the Daytona 500, Michael Waltrip, Darrell Waltrip's thirty-seven-year-old baby brother, off on a victory lap in his yellow NAPA No. 15 car, happier than happy after capturing the biggest stock car race in all Creation, first win in his life in his 463rd race . . . look at another spot on the track and there was Dale.

Was he all right?

The monitors in the control truck blinked out all the color-camera choices. Happy winner. Happy. Live. Crash on tape. The black No. 3 car is going all right, going all right, wait a minute, nudged, going left, going right—slow it down—that's the No. 36 car, the yellow car, Kenny Schrader, coming in from the side, the M&M's car, hits the No. 3 car and they go into the wall together and, wow, everything flies everywhere. Crash live. The car is back on the grass, rolled down the embankment from the wall. What are they doing? Why isn't Dale crawling out of there? The rescue workers have arrived. Maybe he broke a leg. Maybe the side was caved in. Boy, is he going to be pissed at somebody. Won't he? Where is Dale?

Way too much.

The voices from the truck came through Darrell Waltrip's earpiece and joined the voice in his head. Dale will be fine. Dale has been in about a billion of these crashes, much worse than this one. If he comes out of that car soon enough, we may even get a word with him. Won't that be a hoot? The eyes of Waltrip, a fifty-four-year-old man who had driven for thirty years, won 84 races and three Winston Cup championships, knew better. They had seen just about all of the good things and all of the bad that can happen on a racetrack. This was bad.

"This is bad," he told the voices in the truck.

The other color man in the booth, Larry McReynolds, was pretty much speechless. He didn't know what to say. This was his debut as a color commentator after a lifetime of work as a race car mechanic. For two years in his career, he had been Dale Earnhardt's crew chief. He trained his binoculars on the activity around the mangled No. 3 car down the track, the car he once had treated with the same love and care he gave his children, and found himself paralyzed by the inner debate.

"Schrader is looking in the car . . . backing off in a hurry . . . that's not good . . . oh, could be anything . . . maybe Dale's unconscious. . . .

"The emergency crew is reaching inside, working on him . . . that could be something bad. No, that could be anything. . . .

"The emergency crew is cutting off the roof . . . that's not good . . . then, again, it's standard procedure. If Dale broke something. . . .

"They're putting him on a stretcher, taking him to the ambulance . . . OK, that's standard procedure. . . .

"They're covering up the car. . . .

"The ambulance is not going very fast. . . .

Shit.

The idea that the greatest driver in NASCAR history could crash and die on the final turn of the final lap of the biggest race on the NASCAR schedule simply did not compute. Especially if that driver was Dale Earnhardt.

———

They were all new, the members of this Fox crew, at what is billed as "The Great American Race." They had been put together, collected, in the past year for the debut of NASCAR on the network. Fox had paid an unprecedented $1.6 billion to televise just half of the NASCAR season every year for the next eight years. The Daytona 500, the annual stock car Super Bowl, was the most important part of the package.

Everyone was nervous. No, not nervous, really, but excited. More than two hundred people were involved in the telecast.

"The idea was that we were moving into a new era of motorsports coverage," Fox producer Neil Goldberg says. "We were doing some things in production that never had been done. Our team was close to the size of a team that would cover a Super Bowl."

A sequence of robotic cameras had been installed around the 2.5-mile track, so that for the first time an entire race could be covered from a low, street-corner angle. The biggest problem in televising race cars in the past was capturing the speed, the concept of how fast these cars were really traveling. This would help. Microphones, placed strategically, could be left open to capture the accompanying roar.

A moving scroll, the Fox Box, had been invented for the top inch of the screen to keep viewers abreast of the always-changing standings. A computer tracking device, Fox Trax, could superimpose arrows onto the screen, pointing to any number of moving cars. All this was laid upon the existing angles and features of traditional coverage, the shots from the blimp, the interviews from pit road, the sight of nervous wives chewing their well-done nails while their husbands flew around the track at close to 200 miles per hour.

The coverage, the attention, was a testament to how much this one-time regional sport featuring good ol' boys banging their look-alike Fords and Chevrolets and Pontiacs and Hudson Hornets into one another had grown. NASCAR was national. NASCAR was modern. NASCAR was now. Giant concrete speedways had popped like so many carbuncles across the map of America, megastadiums that sat more than 100,000 people on a Sunday afternoon, hordes of true belivers in racing and speed.

While the ratings numbers for the traditional four big professional sports—football, baseball, basketball, and hockey—were in a sodden decline, NASCAR ratings were a skyrocket. NASCAR was NASDAQ, at least the NASDAQ of a couple years earlier. The merchandise flew off the shelves. The most famous corporate names in the country—Procter and Gamble and Coke and Pepsi and Budweiser, the King of Beers—fought each other to place their ads on the cars. The drivers, drawn now from across the country, had become spokesmen and stars, the last large band of American white boys left on the athletic scene after football and basketball had gone black and baseball had gone Hispanic and hockey was filled with European names that would get you a lot of points in a good game of Scrabble.

NASCAR! They look like you! They talk like you! This unspoken thought could not be denied. An increasing portion of the white, mainstream public was settling down behind the steering wheels of these colorful, highly tuned racing machines and driving away on a vicarious 500-mile Sunday afternoon. The newly inaugurated President, George W. Bush, was known to be a NASCAR man. Yes, he was.

"I'll tell you how much this has grown," Goldberg, the producer, says. "I started working in auto racing, television, in 1982 for ESPN. In the mid-eighties, we'd go to Bristol, this little half-mile track in the mountains of Tennessee, and there'd be maybe 20,000 people in the stands. We go there now, there are seats for 160,000 people and they're all filled. It's just been amazing to see."

Goldberg, forty-two years old, originally from Sudbury, Massachusetts, had fallen in love with the sport. The races were terrific, he thought, but the people were even better. Even as the scene had grown larger, the businessmen in suits running more and more aspects of the operation, the people at the base level were different from the people in all other sports. There was a purity to them. They were a collection of success stories, all of them, no-nonsense dreamers who sacrificed and fought to wind up in the spotlight. There was a humility mixed with ambition that could not be denied.

"These are people . . . you don't go to school to play auto racing," Goldberg says. "Every other sport, you can play it at your school. You want to play football? You play it at the school. Basketball? Same thing. If you want to be in auto racing, you have to go somewhere after school. Or you have to leave school. You hang around garages, racetracks, making yourself useful, looking for your break. You go down to one of the NASCAR teams and try to get a job. No other sport demands so much determination."

The only moments when Goldberg had questioned his love for the game had been when the game had turned sour, when a car had flown out of control, when a driver had slumped against the wheel, when the ambulance had arrived and the news was not good. They were infrequent, these moments, but they happened often enough. Goldberg would wonder about his job. Was he encouraging some deadly pastime? Was he spreading good words about an inherently bad enterprise? What was he doing? The people of racing always brought him back.

"The people are wonderful," he says. "They are so infectious with their enthusiasm. It's hard to walk away. Even now, as different as this sport has become with all this money, these people are you and me. You sit down with them for an hour and you have the feeling you've made a friend. Can you do that if you sit in the locker room of the Los Angeles Lakers? You can do that here. The people are so great."

The idea, lying underneath all the technological bells and whistles, was to show how great these people really were. And the greatest of them all was Dale Earnhardt.

"He was in a unique position," Goldberg says. "He was the bridge, the connector between the old days of auto racing and the new NASCAR. He was the old-school race driver who ushered in the modern era, the hard-nosed driver moved into the present."

Forty-nine years old, winner of seven Winston Cup championships to tie King Richard Petty for the all-time record, he was the success story to top all of the other success stories, a multimillionaire who had come from nowhere and nothing to rule his sport. He had a smile that could light up an orphanage. He had a stare that could melt a spark plug. He was a man's man, a hunter and fisherman, a family man who asked for no favors and gave no ground.

In twenty-one years on the Winston Cup circuit, he had dented more fenders, caused more controversy than any dozen drivers you could find. The only group that sometimes seemed as large as his fans was his enemies. The four tractor-trailers selling his souvenirs at the racetrack every week usually sold more merchandise than the trailers of all the other drivers combined.

The joke was that schoolchildren in his home state of North Carolina learned to count by saying "1–2–Dale Earnhardt–4–5–6–7–8–9–10." That was how famous he was. His black No. 3 car was his armor and tool on the racetrack, an extension of his hard-bitten personality. He took no prisoners, never had, never would. He was a constant Clint Eastwood, taking care of the bad guys and picking up that fistful of dollars at the end. He was old and still good and still hip, a phenomenon right there in American culture.

He was the star. He was the star of NASCAR stars, his success and life almost a mirror of the great growth of the sport. He was—that most overused and misused of all phrases, but absolutely true here—an American icon.

"You're driving home and the traffic's stopped up and you're just sitting there," H. A. Humpy Wheeler, president of Lowe's Motor Speedway in Charlotte, says. "You do that five days a week and you're sick of it. You live your life by rules. You wear a tie. You work for a guy you don't like.

"For once, you'd like to break the rules. You'd like to get in a race car and just go wherever you wanted, get past all of those other people, doing what you want to do. Well, maybe you can't do that, but you can go to the racetrack on the weekend and watch somebody else do it. You can watch Dale Earnhardt. He breaks the rules."

Subtlety never had been part of his modus operandi. He conceded nothing. Are you looking at me? That's right. You. He had old-time values, working under an old-time code. Nothing scared him. Nothing stopped him. There was an engaging kick-ass toughness about him that had been there from the beginning and simply would not leave.

Fox had plans for Dale Earnhardt.

"Oh, we had things all set up, Dale and me," Darrell Waltrip says. "I had this sound effect—the sound they played when the shark appeared in *Jaws*—that I was going to use every time he came up from behind on someone. We had a bunch of stuff. We'd already talked about it."

The presence of Waltrip in the booth opened up all kinds of roads with Earnhardt. Retired only at the end of the 2000 season, the well-spoken Waltrip served as nemesis and rival during Earnhardt's early years, fighting him to the wire for championships. Called to replace the injured Steve Park in 1998 in the Pennzoil car fielded by Dale Earnhardt Incorporated (DEI), Earnhardt's race team, Waltrip became ally and friend. A lot of experiences, a lot of time, had been shared. Waltrip called Earnhardt "my frenemy—90 percent friend and 10 percent enemy."

"I think the time I spent driving for him in 1998 really changed things between us," Waltrip says. "Any hard feelings disappeared. I was helping him out and he was helping me out. We were able to let our guard down and just talk. It wasn't all about 'you wrecked me' or 'I wrecked you.' We could talk about anything."

The plans already were working. The Fox crew televised just about every race or qualifying session during Speed Week at Daytona, shaking the bugs out, learning how everybody worked together, getting ready for the big race on Sunday. Earnhardt was a main attraction.

"He knew how it all worked," Goldberg says. "You'd do a live shot and he'd come in from the side, unexpected, and grab the announcer. He'd grab a Sharpie and walk up to the camera and sign his autograph right on the camera lens. He worked great with Darrell. You could see the rapport. He came up to Matt Yokum, our reporter, after qualifying and grabbed Matt's headset and said, 'Let me talk to Waltrip.' And they talked. Just these two guys who knew so much about racing. I think about it now, they talked every day during our telecasts. Darrell even argued with him about wearing the open-faced helmet, about his choice of safety equipment."

The plot possibilities with Earnhardt for the big day were endless. Waltrip's brother, Michael, now was the third driver for the DEI team, his first chance at handling a truly competitive car. Park, the driver Darrell once replaced, was back in the Pennzoil car as the No. 2 driver for DEI. The top driver was Earnhardt's son, Dale Junior, twenty-six years old and already successful, already a threat.

Earnhardt himself, revitalized after disc surgery a year and a half earlier, second in the Winston Cup standings in 2000, was in the familiar No. 3 Monte Carlo of Richard Childress Racing. This was a driver/owner partnership that had lasted through seventeen successful seasons. Why change it now? Earnhardt felt as confident as he ever had. The storied Daytona track, the scene of his greatest win in 1998 after going a bizarre 0-for-19 in the 500 for the bulk of his career, surely was a character. Larry McReynolds was the crew chief for that race. He would have stories about Earnhardt. Waltrip, the competitor, friend, frenemy, would have stories.

Throw in the return of Dodge to Daytona, two Dodges sitting in the front row at the start. Throw in baby-faced Jeff Gordon, the clinician, the successful driving opposite of Earnhardt. Throw in pit stops and blown engines, restrictor plates and airfoils to keep everyone close, defending champion Bobby Labonte and the rest of the field, 175,000 fans and the sight of Florida sun for the good folks back north in the scraggly days of winter.

How good could all this be?

"We were eleven seconds from having the greatest telecast in the history of the Daytona 500," Neil Goldberg says. "That's how close we came."

The black car and the three cars that the driver of the black car owned were in the middle of the action for the entire day. Earnhardt was the leader on the 27th of the 200 laps, holding the lead for 11 before being passed by Childress teammate Mike Skinner. Earnhardt was the leader on laps 83 and 84, then dropped back again. This was the restrictor-plate mayhem, speeds legislated into uniformity, that Earnhardt always said he hated but always handled very well, racing in packs, two wide, three wide, different grooves on the banked track. Earnhardt was always involved.

Early in the race, fender to fender, he bumped with rookie Kurt Busch. He appeared to turn and—wait a minute, the Fox cameras caught it—he stuck his left hand out the driver's-side window and raised the middle finger to Kurt Busch. In the middle of the race! The finger! Flying!

"I remember thinking that he was going to be talking to Kurt Busch after this race," Goldberg says. "He wasn't going to be angry. I didn't think so. He was going to be like a father, giving advice to a son."

On the 174th lap, the perils of restrictor-plate racing arrived. Robby Gordon hit Ward Burton and Ward Burton hit Tony Stewart and Tony Stewart went flying. This was a spectacular crash that eventually involved nineteen cars, almost half the starting field. Stewart's car spun and flipped twice, *badda-boom, badda-boom,* crashing into teammate Bobby Labonte on the way. The pictures of the orange Home Depot car going through the air were perfect television. Looked bad, wasn't bad. This was almost a Hollywood-stunt-driver kind of crash.

"If you didn't know anything about auto racing, you would have thought that was the bad crash," Goldberg says. "If you knew auto racing, though, you knew that the speed was dissipating as Stewart was going over and over. Flipping was good. That energy was being used up. The bad crashes are the ones where the car at great speed hits an object that doesn't move. That's when there's no chance for the energy to go anywhere."

Earnhardt, riding low and ahead of Stewart, missed the entire jackpot. When the race was restarted on lap 180, he was second behind Dale Jr., first on lap 183, then fell behind Michael Waltrip on lap 184.

With five laps to go, he was third behind Waltrip and Dale Jr. What could be better?

"I wonder sometimes what the NASCAR of the future will be like," Humpy Wheeler says. "It'll clearly be different. One of the things I wonder about . . . did you ever see the Tour de France, the bicycle race? They run that in teams, the rest of the team helping one driver to victory. Maybe that's where we're going. There never have been the number of teams there are today. Maybe that's what we'll see in NASCAR."

Maybe this was the start. In a Twin 125 qualifying race during the week, Earnhardt was leading when a bunch of cars stormed past him on the final turn, using the draft from his car to speed up and slip free. That seemed to be the way the cars worked for this new season. Wouldn't drivers try to do the same thing in this race?

There seemed to be little doubt that Earnhardt thought that would be happening again as he approached the final turn. He advised both Waltrip and Dale Jr. to ride on the low part of the racetrack. He put himself into a blocking mode, slowing just enough to stop the hard chargers in the pack behind him from making a final run at the front. The move was nothing less than a basketball pick, freeing his teamates—employees, really, one of them his son—to roll to the basket.

The problem with a basketball pick is that sometimes the defender, trying to catch his man, bumps into the man throwing the pick. The bump here was at 185 miles per hour. It came from Sterling Marlin from behind and sent Earnhardt's car to the left, toward the apron for a moment. Then the car turned hard right and went on a straight line until it crashed into the wall at the same time it was hit by Schrader's car on the door of the passenger's side.

What exactly happened? What? There would be controversy and questions in the future:

Did Earnhardt overcorrect the steering in the second after the impact?

Did he have no control, none?

Had he put himself in peril by slowing down the way he did instead of following the hard-charging, no-surrender course he had used during his entire career?

Would he have been better served with the full helmet that all of the other drivers use instead of the half-helmet he insisted on wearing?

Should he have been using HANS, a head and neck support system that recently had been developed?

Did his seat belt break?

There would be press conferences and the potential for lawsuits. Claims and counterclaims. The rescue workers who arrived at the car would become momentarily famous, telling their stories on television. Sterling Marlin would receive death threats and shut off his Web site. Doctors would be questioned. Experts would be hired. An entire country would be shaken.

None of that was known in the broadcast booth. There was only the sight of what had happened.

"TV does not do that [crash] justice," Waltrip said into his microphone after watching the replay at the same time as viewers. "That is incredible impact. Those are the kind of accidents that are absolutely frightening."

The head still battled the eyes. Maybe . . . You never know . . . Maybe. Goldberg, in the truck, couldn't get the thought out of his mind that somewhere Earnhardt was going to pop out of a door, pop out of the ambulance, pop out as a smiling jack-in-the-box. Waltrip thought that maybe he should say more, that this was what he was being paid to do, give his analysis, but what if you said the fateful words and they were wrong? Half the television stations in the country had killed off driver Ernie Irvan after a crash at Michigan and Ernie Irvan was walking and talking and probably eating dinner right now. Caution had to be the guide.

The telecast was scheduled to end at five o'clock and David Hill, head of Fox Sports, was in the studio and said the schedule would be followed. What more could be said if nobody knew the answer for certain to the awful question? An answer might take a long time to arrive. The broadcast ended with Dale Earnhardt still alive at five and—later reports said—Dale Earnhardt was pronounced dead at 5:16 at Halifax Medical Center. The rescue workers and doctor at the track later said that they were sure he was dead while he was still in the car.

He had suffered a basal skull fracture, eight broken ribs on his left side, a broken left ankle, a fractured breastbone and collarbone, and hip abrasions. The basal skull fracture, the newest fear of race car drivers, had killed him. The whole thing, even listing the injuries, one after another, seemed almost beyond belief.

There are moments—more and more of them, really, in modern life—where the real becomes so outrageous that it outstrips the fictional. *If I saw that in the movies or on television, I wouldn't believe it!* Some nitwit named McVeigh fills a Ryder truck with fertilizer and blows up a government building in Oklahoma City, killing 168 people. A six-year-old kid named Elian with puppy-dog brown eyes is pulled out of the waters off Florida, his mother drowned in an escape attempt from Cuba, and it becomes an international incident. A football player named O.J., maybe the most recognizable football player of all, is accused of killing his wife and leads an entire city's police force on a motorized chase through the freeways of Los Angeles. These are plots a hundred screenwriters in a hundred lonely rooms couldn't imagine, too weird for the conventional mind to accept, too flat-out unbelievable.

The death of Dale Earnhardt was one of these moments. Dozens of analogies would be made. What if Michael Jordan dropped dead, going to the foul line with a second left in the seventh and final game of the NBA Finals? What if Tiger Woods were hit by lightning, standing over the final birdie putt on the 18th green, 72nd hole of the Masters at Augusta? What if? What if the President of the United States said "I do" to finish out his inauguration and keeled forward? What if any of these unbeliev-able things happened? Would they have been more shocking than this one?

This was the ultimate public death of an ultimate public figure. The Nielsen rating was 10.1, the highest number in the history of Daytona 500 coverage.

Waltrip was supposed to go to Victory Lane to see his brother. He had a friend, a Daytona policeman, who was going to escort him through the crowd. The policeman's wife worked at Halifax Medical Center. She called her husband and told him that Waltrip should come to the hospital. Waltrip went, talked with Earnhardt's wife, Teresa, and members of the family, then returned to the condo he had rented to be with his own wife, Stevie. She had been close with Earnhardt, had taped a Bible verse on the steering column of his car before the race, a tradition. Waltrip and his wife talked for a while and then went back to the track. His brother, Michael, was still there, not really knowing what to do. Darrell says that four months later, his brother still does not know what to do. It is a shame.

Larry McReynolds left after the race to catch a plane. The airport is across the street from the speedway, so he walked, still keeping up the internal debate between his head and his eyes. By the time his cell phone rang, while he ate dinner in the airport cafeteria, Neil Goldberg on the line, he was ready for the grim news. The eyes had won.

Goldberg stayed at work in the truck. The decision was made that the death of Dale Earnhardt would not be announced on the air until it was offically announced to the media. This happened at 7 P.M. when NASCAR president Mike Helton stood in the front of the pressroom and said, "This is understandably the hardest announcement I've ever had to make. We've lost Dale Earnhardt." Goldberg stayed at the controls as Fox Sportsnet ran a special report. A number of people were crying.

"Covering the Winston Cup, you really get to know the people," Goldberg says. "You're with them every week. It isn't like other sports, where you can go in and cover two teams and maybe never see them again for an entire season. You're with the forty-three teams of NASCAR for the whole year. Friendships are made. You get close to people you like."

At nine o' clock, a studio show called *Victory Lane* premiered on Fox Sportsnet from a set in Charlotte, North Carolina. The host was sportscaster John Roberts, and his color commentator was Derrike Cope, a driver. The same pressures, Fox executives hovering in the background, new contract, new approach, had been present all day. The same sadness crept into the room when the news was official about what had happened in Daytona.

Derrike Cope had won the Daytona 500 in 1990, beating Earnhardt on the last lap when Earnhardt's tire fell apart. They were linked forever by that moment. His wife was a friend of Earnhardt's wife.

"It was a struggle to get a show together, but everyone was very professional," John Roberts says. "We put together a tribute. We went to the files, not knowing what we were going to find, but there was some wonderful videotape."

Yes there was.

For sure.

Wonderful videotape.

2

AT THE ALTAR

Chuck Thompson knew before the television networks announced the news. He had a friend who was a friend of the Earnhardt family. Kannapolis, North Carolina, is a small place, and the friend got a call and made a call and Chuck Thompson heard and started thinking.

"I told my wife I wanted to do something," he says. "I just wasn't sure what it was."

He still wasn't sure the next morning when he climbed the ladder to the sign in front of his store, Honeycutt Furniture, right there on South Cannon Boulevard, no more than three blocks from where Dale Earnhardt was raised. The sign was one of those adjustable deals, a low-cost version of a theater marquee, with black plastic letters that could be moved around against a white background to change a message. Chuck Thompson started writing in black plastic letters.

"One thing I wanted to do was include Neil Bonnett," he says. "Everyone knows Neil was Dale's best friend and also died in a crash at Daytona. I started writing and kept going until I ran out of room."

The final message was:

GOODBYE DALE—3
TELL DAVEY NEIL
ALAN ADAM & KENNY
HELLO FOR US

The words captured the sport's most recent sad moments. Included, in addition to Bonnett, were NASCAR drivers Davey Allison, Alan Kulwicki, Adam Petty, and Kenny Irwin, who all lost their lives early. Thompson is a NASCAR fan.

"I never met Dale," he says. "His mother, Martha, and his brother, Ralph, have been customers, but Dale shopped up the street at Tucker Furniture. There's a story. About eighteen, nineteen years ago, he still had a tab at Tucker Furniture. He was paying it off, something like ten bucks a week. Think about that and how far he came."

Thompson planned to remove the sign on Earnhardt's birthday, but May had arrived and the sign remained. He said he simply couldn't bring himself to take it down.

BEGINNINGS

The woods always awaited. The farmland always awaited. The outdoors. Toward the end he was on some outrageous public treadmill most of the time, the speeds ratcheted higher and higher—"Gotta go" were the two words Dale Earnhardt said more than any others on a daily basis. "Gotta go, gotta go"—but when he came back to Cabarrus and Rowan and Iredell counties in North Carolina his feet were on familiar red clay and his body slowed down to a pace where he could hear his own heartbeat.

He was a creature of this land. This was what he knew.

He walked the same woods he walked when he was ten years old. He hid in the same trees. He stalked the grandchildren and great-grandchildren and great-great-grandchildren of the white-tailed deer he had stalked as a child. The equipment changed, the rifles more expensive and the boots and camouflage clothing top of the line, but the game never changed. The deer hid. The human being sought.

"You want to go tomorrow?" he would say on the phone to his uncle, Dub Coleman. Or to a boyhood friend. Or to someone else who was close, familiar, real.

Sure.

The patterns of a lifetime would be followed. Clothes would be matched to the environment, shirts and pants and jackets and boots and hats packed in a box for a night with pinecones and leaves to remove all human smells. The big breakfast would be skipped. No need to send out a warning signal of ham and eggs and flapjacks. The deer had senses tuned to detect the slightest irregularities, the smallest tickle to the eye, the ear, the nose. The human being had to keep those tickles to a minimum.

This was a game of nuance, of subtlety. Funny, perhaps, that a man who made a fortune in a brash and noisy business full of speed and horsepower and standing ovations would find such pleasure in the quiet. Then again, perhaps not. Maybe this was the foundation of all that success, the bedrock. Maybe this was the edge. Know the deer. Know nature. Know yourself. Know the game, any game.

High in a tree, waiting and waiting and waiting some more, waiting for the whole day if necessary, the seven-time Winston Cup champion was as alone as he was in that race car, responsible to no one but himself, making his own decisions about life and death. NASCAR once did a study of drivers' heart rates at the start of a race. The average driver's heart beat a hundred times per minute. Earnhardt's beat fifty-three times. He would wait. The deer would follow patterns they had set in the ground, prints and scratch marks that indicated where they liked to go. The human being would be there to disrupt those patterns.

"Dale had an uncanny ability to remain still," his uncle Dub says. "His father had the same ability. The two of them, I don't know how they did it. The other thing they had—both of them—was great peripheral vision. They could see things from the corners of their eyes that no one else could see."

As he became famous, the driver with his picture on the front of a Wheaties box had chances to hunt and fish anywhere he wanted. He went up and down the continent, traveling with famous hunters and experienced guides, tracking exotic birds and animals, bringing them home from the taxidermist stuffed with a perpetual smile. He appeared on hunting and fishing television shows. He endorsed equipment. He still came back to the familiar woods.

"This must be awful small-time for you now," his uncle suggested one afternoon a couple of years ago. "After the places you've been."

"Not at all," Dale Earnhardt replied. "I love this as much as I ever have. There's nothing like stalking the North Carolina white-tailed deer."

This was home.

———

He was born on April 29, 1951, in Kannapolis, a small city twenty miles northeast of Charlotte, the first son and third child of Ralph and Martha Earnhardt. Kannapolis essentially was where he stayed for his entire life. Even when he broke free, famous and rich, he strayed no farther than ten miles down Route 136, the Mooresville Road, to build the log home of his dreams and his elaborate business empire on nine hundred acres of farmland in Mooresville. Kannapolis always was important. Kannapolis was where the real score was kept.

He was a lint head who made a mark.

"'Lint heads' is what the people over in Concord call the people from Kannapolis," former city mayor Richard Anderson says. "Concord always was the seat of the county government, supposedly more educated and refined. Kannapolis was the mill town. For the longest time, until 1984, we were the largest unincorporated city in America. We didn't even have a city government. The county ran all of our affairs.

"The rich kids against the lint heads. That would be the big football game at the end of our season, when we sent A. L. Brown High School out to play against Concord."

The easily used term "mill town," attached to a string of cities and towns across the state, wasn't descriptive enough for Kannapolis. The city, with a population of 36,000, now is pretty much a bedroom suburb of Charlotte, the mill tied up in bankruptcy proceedings, but when Earnhardt was being raised, the mill *was* the town. The town *was* the mill. The mill was the very reason the town existed.

When industrialist D. A. Cannon, sick of sending southern-picked cotton north to be turned into fabric, decided to build his mill on a stretch of Carolina farmland in 1906, he had to build a town with it. He chose a Greek word for "City of Looms," laid out a grid with the mill in the middle, and proceeded to construct his view of a utopian, profitable paradise.

The Cannon Mills, pumping out Cannon towels and Fieldcrest sheets and assorted other fabrics, soon dominated the previously agricultural landscape. The buildings were big and utilitarian, giant redbrick boxes that belched smoke into the tarheel blue sky. They had no-nonsense names like "Plant 1" and "Plant 2," and an around-the-clock schedule. The town that Cannon added was also utilitarian, street upon street of matched wooden boxes. The mill controlled all the boxes. The mill controlled the lives.

Work at one pay level and you were allowed to rent one size house. Work at another pay level and you were allowed to move up to a larger rental. Become a supervisor and you could rent the biggest company houses of all on Ridge Avenue. It was an economic circle. The money paid by the company pretty much was returned directly to the company.

Charles Cannon, D. A.'s son, was the commencement speaker for a number of years at the high school and always would finish his address by promising every graduate a job at the mills. The mills were life itself! The mill donated land and subsidized extras for the school system. The mill backed the building of the Cabarrus County Hospital. The mill brought in the YMCA. When 5,000 of the mill's workers went to World War II, Charles promised housing upon return. More boxes, called "the GI homes," were added to the grid.

"The mill took care of all of your basic needs," Anderson says. "They painted your house every three years. They took care of the roof. You didn't even have to mow your lawn. The company sent crews through, once a week, to mow everybody's lawn. The electricians, the plumbers, any service you could think of . . . the mill provided that. When the company finally ran into trouble in the eighties and sold off all the homes, people truly didn't know what to do. They never had owned a house before. They didn't know what to do when the toilet broke. It was quite a situation for a while."

On the edges of the grid, other houses were built through the years as a service economy developed, as people saved and wanted to own their own little piece of America. A lack of originality—or maybe too much originality—was used when these new neighborhoods developed and streets were named. Each area seemed to have a general theme. There was a section of streets named after women's first names ("Debbie" and "Betty" and "Evelyn" and "Hazel") and another named after the tales of Robin Hood ("Nottingham" and "Sherwood" and "Longbow") and another after states ("Kentucky" and "Texas" and "Michigan" and "Florida").

On the north side of the grid, a section called "Car Town" was created. The streets were named after the brands or models of cars at the time. There was a "Buick" and a "Hudson" and a "DeSoto" and a "Cadillac" and a "Plymouth" and a "Dodge" and a "Chrysler." There was also a "V-8 Street" and a "Coach" and a "Sedan." This was where the Earnhardts lived.

When Dale was born, they were in a two-bedroom apartment on Coach, all the kids in one bedroom, but soon the family moved to 1412 Sedan Avenue at the corner of Coach. This was where Dale grew up with his older sisters, Kaye and Kathy, and his younger brothers, Randy and Danny, in a white frame house in a modest neighborhood, the house where his mother, Martha, still lives, trophies lined up across the living room walls.

If he had been born ten blocks closer to the mills, NASCAR historians could note that Dale Earnhardt was born on Chevrolet. Then again, if he were born only nine blocks closer, he would have been born on Ford.

Ralph Earnhardt was also born in Kannapolis, twenty-two years before his first son. His parents were farmers, and he married Martha Coleman from Concord, the daughter of farmers. The couple started a family young, and Ralph followed the other lint heads to the mills. Martha took a job at a downtown diner near the mills. That seemed to be the natural progression of Kannapolis life. Ralph had dropped out of school in the sixth grade.

"Everybody worked in the mills at some time," Dub, Martha's brother, says. "That's how you started. I was there, myself, until they lied to me one day. They lied, and I said, 'That's it, I'm going home.' I remember the supervisor said, 'You can't do that.' I said, 'Yes, I can.'

The very next day I got a job hanging steel. I never even missed a day's pay. It was the best move I ever made.

"Ralph had a second job, helping out in a garage. He knew a lot about cars. The guy who owned the shop had a race car. Ralph put a big Cadillac engine in it for him. The guy got sick or something one time, and Ralph drove a couple of races. I guess that was it for Ralph in the mills. He was hooked on racing."

The choice of addiction turned out to be wonderful. The surrounding area long had been a hotbed for baseball—the most famous Kannapolis native at the time was Billy Goodman, a solid third baseman for the Boston Red Sox in the fifties—but auto racing now challenged as the No. 1 local sport. The crowds that once would stand on the lawn outside Whitley's Funeral Home and listen to a special broadcast of the local American Legion team's faraway crusade through the state baseball tournament now were lured to small, dusty, dirt tracks that gradually had sprung up everywhere.

"You have to understand the geography," Humpy Wheeler, sort of the poet laureate of stock-car racing, says. "This is the Piedmont, a stretch of red clay that goes up roughly from Birmingham, Alabama, into Virginia. There is no better dirt for a racetrack than the red clay of the Piedmont. If you were a farmer and you had a dozer to make everything level, you pretty much could build yourself a racetrack. There were a lot of trees, so there was lumber everywhere. If you had a friend who had a sawmill, you could get yourself some boards for fences and bleachers. Dig a few holes for latrines and you were in business.

"This was a different time, though, from today. This was a mean time around here. There was a lot of poverty, the mills starting to cut back, and poverty brings meaness. Going to a race wasn't like going to a race now. There were a lot of fights, a lot of drinking. Racetracks were places of retribution. People brought up in this environment were constantly trying to get out of it. Racetracks were a way to escape."

Everything definitely was minor league. Racing, itself, was minor league. The only race that counted nationally was the Indianapolis 500, which featured expensive, open-cockpit cars and the few famous drivers of the time. The rest of the races, whether on dirt or on asphalt, were stock-car affairs, half the equipment salvaged from the local junkyard, towed to the track in back of a family truck, grease still on the work clothes of the men who got out of the truck and then behind the wheel of the race car.

The NASCAR circuit was just beginning, the beach at Daytona already an important place to be in February, but racing in the South mostly was chaos. Standings and statistics and overall championships were sketchy. Every night there were races someplace. A driver could pick and choose where to go. On weekends, there were a lot of choices. Racers just raced, showing up here and there and wherever. This was the grassroots of what was to come, but it wasn't something being carefully cultivated inside some window box. This was crabgrass and dandelions, just popping from the soil.

Into the middle of it all came Ralph.

He was a curious and quiet figure in a noisy time. The people who knew him use the old film star Gary Cooper to fill out their description. Gary Cooper in the dusty street, slapping leather in *High Noon*. Or maybe in a trench in France in *Sergeant York*. Ralph Earnhardt was a lone rider, quiet and precise and very, very good at what he did.

There was a stubbornness and individualism to him that was immediately visible. His first daughter was five months old when he quit the mill to go racing, just did, and he went from there. His wife was nineteen. He resembled nothing so much as some automotive farmer, some grease-monkey sharecropper, pouring his heart and soul into his crop and hoping that the rain and sun would arrive in proper sequence. The difference was that his harvests came four and five nights a week.

"Ralph was different from most of the drivers around the dirt tracks those days," Humpy Wheeler says. "Most drivers had jobs. They raced on the weekends. Racing was Ralph's job. That's what he did. He didn't drive like Dale did, all out all the time. He couldn't afford to. He was driving the family bank. Ralph would just drive for position for three quarters of a race. You wouldn't even hear his name. Then, as it got to the end, there he was. He was like some apparition out of the clouds. You'd wonder where he came from. He couldn't afford to wreck, you see. He had to drive that way."

He would build and tune his cars in the cinder-block garage he built in the back of the house on Sedan Street. He would tow the car to the track from the back of his truck. He would run the race, make money or not, tow the car home. He was the ultimate small businessman.

"He'd build the chassis, build the engine, then get in the car and race it," David Oliver, who once was married to one of Ralph Earnhardt's daughters, Kathy, says. "You can't do any more than that, build the car from nothing and then race it. Dale got to be that way, too. He didn't have to do it, of course, but he could have broken down a car and put it back together. I'll bet there aren't a lot of them in NASCAR today who could do that."

Ralph was so precise, he seemed wrapped in an air of mystery. When he arrived at a track, his car was ready to race. End of story. The other drivers and mechanics would fidget and fret, making last-minute adjustments until the cars were called onto the track. Ralph would smoke a cigarette. If he didn't like something with his car, well, he simply would pack up and go home.

There was a famous story: During one season, everyone driving Fords was using a truck rear end which had a small part, the axle key, that kept breaking. Ford had not made the part strong enough to withstand the demands of racing. The only driver who never had problems was Ralph Earnhardt. During a two-month period, he seemed to win everything and never broke an axle key. How did he do it? Finally, someone somehow learned the secret. Ralph had taken a certain model Craftsman screwdriver of a certain size, cut off the top and the end, and fashioned a stronger, better, unbreakable axle key. The rest of the drivers hurried to the nearest Sears store in Charlotte, the only distributor of Craftsman tools, to buy the screwdriver of that certain model and certain size.

"I'm sorry," the Sears salesman said. "I can give you any other size screwdriver but that one. There's some guy from Kannapolis comes down here and buys every one of 'em I have. I don't know what he does with them."

"He was just an interesting guy, Ralph," Humpy Wheeler says. "Taciturn. To a fault. I was working with Firestone tires at the time. I hired him to do some tests for us. He'd go out and come back and I'd ask about the tires. If he said, 'OK,' that meant they were absolutely great. If he said, 'Had a little problem,' that meant they were awful. He was a man of few words."

———

Dink Widenhouse was part of Ralph Earnhardt's competition, another driver in the dirt. He also was one of Ralph's friends. They rode together a bunch of times to different tracks, especially to Columbia, South Carolina, on Thursday nights. They'd travel the 100 miles down, bang fenders for a couple of hundred laps in the feature, then drive the 100 miles back, stopping at the same diner on the way so many times it became known to them and everyone else as "Earnhardt's Diner."

The quiet man would talk a bit during these trips because there wasn't much else to do. He had more words for people he knew. The quiet man could unleash a quirky, inquiring mind.

"He pulls out a stopwatch on one of these trips," Widenhouse says. "It wasn't like the stopwatches today, which are part of a normal watch. This was a biscuit watch, just a stopwatch. He says to me—I'm driving—'Widenhouse, you're pretty good with time. Do you think you could tell me how long a minute is without looking at a watch?' I told him I thought I could come pretty close. He says, 'Tell me when to start.'"

Widenhouse sneaked a peek at his odometer and waited until the zero came around. He made sure the speed was at exactly 60 miles an hour. "OK, start your watch up, boy," he said. Earnhardt kept talking, making sure Widenhouse wasn't keeping track by counting numbers in his head. Widenhouse gladly responded. When he noticed the odometer hit zero again, he said, "Time." Earnhardt's stopwatch had recorded exactly one minute.

"He says, 'Damn, Widenhouse, you're good at this,'" Widenhouse says. "I never did tell him how I did it."

Widenhouse was driving just to drive. He sold trucks and truck parts, same job he does today, and drove other people's race cars for the simple adventure, for the competition. He noticed the economics, the fact that a $200 winner's check would just about cover the bill to repair the '37 Ford coupe for the next race. This did not seem like a growth business to him. Racing was a passion, "worse than a drug."

Ralph Earnhardt, it seemed to Widenhouse, was addicted worse than anyone else. A professional race-car driver. Just didn't make sense.

"I'd just go out there hoping to win," Widenhouse says. "If the car was wrecked or broke down, well, that was too bad for the owner. Ralph, he was conservative. You'd watch him, keeping an eye on the pits, trying to see who'd dropped out. Then make his move in the end."

There were reformed bootleggers and active bootleggers in half the other cars, guys who would "drive back from Hickory to Charlotte with a load, faster than they drove in the race." There was dust in the air, fights in the stands, fights in the pits. There was adventure, to be sure.

"Golly, I got banged up at Darlington in 1956," Widenhouse says. "I hit Roy Bentley's car in the middle of the racetrack between the third and fourth turns, and Fireball Roberts, he ran right over me. I flipped upside down, hit the steering wheel, and was knocked out. I cut my chin, and by hanging upside down in the car, the blood from the cut just ran back down my face. I looked like a stuck pig.

"I woke up in the ambulance and Roy Bentley, the guy I hit, he's in there, too. I said, 'That you, Roy? How am I? How do I look?' Roy looks at me and says, 'Real bad.' I was scared to death . . . but all I had was the cut chin. The blood just made it look awful."

Earnhardt and Widenhouse and a third driver in an Earnhardt-prepared car were doing so well at one particular track, winning every week, that the promoter asked them for a break. Couldn't they lose once? Couldn't they let, say, this nice Ned Jarrett guy win a race? The fix was in. The prize money would be split equally four ways.

The three drivers held back. Jarrett went to the front. Easy. Widenhouse was counting his money until he saw Jarrett's car, dead, sitting on the side with some mechanical problem. Then the rain started. Then the race was red-flagged. Then the same three drivers finished 1-2-3. Then the people in the stands started throwing things. It was not a good night.

"You can't fix a race," Widenhouse says. "That's the only time I ever tried and look what happened. You just can't fix a race."

He and his wife, Frances, would do social things with Ralph and Martha. He remembers a night out for dinner, Ralph promising to pay, but spending the entire night saying, "Widenhouse, remember the time . . ." and bringing up times when Widenhouse had put him into a wall or done some other dastardly deed. Finally, after about the fifth "Widenhouse, remember the time . . . ," Widenhouse said, "Earnhardt, you didn't bring me out for dinner. You brought me out to give me hell." Everybody laughed.

"He had fun, Ralph did," Widenhouse says. "He'd have a party if he won a race. I was more quiet. Frances didn't go for that. I come home one night, 3 A.M., after winning at Myrtle Beach, and I yelled, 'Come on, make me some breakfast. Let's celebrate.' Frances said, 'It's three in the morning, I'm not making any breakfast.' I said, 'You don't understand, I won the race.' She said, 'You don't understand, you're HOME now.'

"Frances wouldn't drive in the Powder Puff derbies they had for the wives of drivers, either. Martha drove. Martha rolled Ralph's car in one of them. Yes she did. Martha rolled that car."

Widenhouse finally decided to retire. He didn't want to take another step and go to the superspeedways, because the speeds made him nervous. He wasn't going to make a living with what he was doing. He might as well quit and sell his truck parts.

His final race was in Columbia. He did not finish. He came off a turn, and Earnhardt ran on the inside of him. The two cars bumped and bumped and turned right and flew off the racetrack, side by side. They went through a fence and out into the real world. Widenhouse's car hit a tree and stopped. Earnhardt's finally rolled dead in a parking lot.

Everybody else was still back inside the track. The lights were bright in the night sky. The two men left their cars and walked back together toward the noise and the action.

"You hurt your hand?" Earnhardt asked.

"No, I'm OK," Widenhouse said.

"You hurt your hand. You're rubbing it."

"It just stings. That's all."

Widenhouse never raced again

———————

For a kid, all of this stuff was magic. It was like being the son of a modern, crew-cut Sir Lancelot who always was off on some hopped-up, six-cylinder steed to slay steel dragons. Ralph's nickname even was "Ironheart," a play on his last name, perhaps, but also a tribute to his determination and spirit. What could be better than being the son of someone named Ironheart?

When a race was won in one of those exotic locations—Columbia on a Thursday, Monroe on a Friday, Greenville-Pickens on a Saturday—Ralph and his one-man pit crew, Uncle Dub, would return home and great smells would come out of the kitchen and everyone would stay up half the night discussing the race. Who wouldn't want to be part of that?

Dale always would recall his childhood in idyllic terms. There was a sweetness to his memories. Ralph was not the hands-on, hug-and-kiss dad of today's suburbs—and Dale would not be that, either—but he was honest and available. A pat on the head or a smile had to be earned the same way a good whack on the rear had to be earned. The choice was up to his kids.

The Car Town neighborhood was something out of *To Kill a Mockingbird,* southern and slow and basic. Even now, a giant Walgreens no more than half a mile away, there is a soft touch to the place, as if you are waiting for someone's mother to bring out a wash to a clothesline or to place an apple pie in a kitchen window to cool. Not a rural environment, perhaps, but not city. Small-town U.S.A. Country.

There were neighborhood bike races, go-kart races, competitions of all kinds. There were football games. There was Sunday school. There were dares and double dares, summer-afternoon leaps into ponds. There always was activity.

"We didn't play baseball, but I remember some softball games," David Oliver says. "There was a field across the street, and we'd mow it and play ball over there. Dale played. Everybody played. Ralph played."

"Dale was kind of a unique kid," his uncle Dub remembers. "One thing he did . . . he could ride a bicycle backwards as well as he could forwards. He'd ride all over the place. Backwards. He'd build his own bikes, too. From an early age, he knew what to do in the garage."

"My cousin, Frank, had a little business, a slot car track, in Midway, which was a section of town," Gregg Dayvault says. "The store was called the D and D. You could bring your slot cars in from home and race 'em on the track. Actually, there were two tracks, a road course and a figure eight. You'd have to pay maybe 25 cents for 15 minutes, 50 cents for a half hour.

"On Friday nights, Frank would hold races. The first trophy Dale Earnhardt ever won for racing was with a slot car at Frank's track. We played everything when we were kids, but you always knew that Dale was mad for racing."

This was not surprising. At home, the garage and the race cars were central to all activity. Men would appear to talk racing and engines with Ralph, to have cars tuned, engines rebuilt. He did work for other people, but his favorite work was for his own machine.

Dale learned the routine of the garage, the places for the tools. He would slip into his father's quiet world and learn whatever he could. From the time he was, say, ten years old, he would be part of the traveling team to the shorter races. Ralph and Dale and Uncle Dub. Uncle Dub would do whatever work there was to do in the pits during a race, cleaning a window or changing a tire by hand, long before the time of the air wrench. Dale would watch from the top of his father's truck. Or over with the sportswriters on top of another truck.

When he didn't make the longer trips, his boundaries constricted by age and school, he would get out of bed early in the morning and go to the garage and try to figure out what had happened in the race. How did the car look? He tried to figure out what had happened by the dents or the dirt or the wear on the tires. He cleaned the car, had it ready, while his father slept late.

This continued into his teenage years, his role in the operation increasing as he grew older. He and then Randy and Danny became the pit crew. Uncle Dub dropped off after a decade of service to raise his own kids. This was the foundation of all that would follow. Working on the cars. Going to the races. This was the family business.

If you look at athletics, you find a string of stars who followed their fathers into the same sport. You see a Kobe Bryant, a Ken Griffey Jr., a Barry Bonds. . . . Was it genetic? Or was it just environmental, being around the game? You look, in fact, at a lot of professions. How often does the accountant's son become an accountant, the doctor's son become a doctor? How often does the son of the grocer, the baker, the barber, the real estate magnate take over the apron, the scissors, the big desk in the corner office? The available path often seems to be the natural path.

Of course, things are never that easy. Hardheaded teenage sons do things that quiet and solid, hardheaded fathers do not like. Earnhardt's thing came when he was sixteen. He quit school. His father, without an education, always preached the virtues of school. Go to school. Stay in school. Don't be a dummy. There is no record that the son was a troublesome student, fighting and brawling, sent to the principal's office time after time. He was an indifferent student. School was boring. Why sit and listen to some gasbag when the world outside was so exciting? Nine grades of this stuff was enough. At sixteen, you're old enough to make up your own mind. Aren't you?

Earnhardt would later regret this decision as much as any he ever made. He would become almost a crusader for staying in school when he became famous and kids listened to him. He would pass the message along to his own sons, shipping Dale Jr. off to military school when Dale Jr. seemed to be an indifferent student. The lack of education always would bother Earnhardt in the future. It bothered his father more when it happened.

"I disappointed my daddy," Earnhardt would say throughout his life. "If I could do one thing over, I'd stay in school. I wouldn't disappoint my daddy."

The son spun off to do the wild-haired things that sixteen-year-old sons do when they quit school and their father is mad at them. The father stayed pissed for a long time. The racing career that probably should have started easier, with Dale just slipping behind the wheel of one of Ralph's well-prepared machines, took a while.

It wasn't until he was nineteen that Dale Earnhardt drove in his first race. He drove his brother-in-law's car.

"I was driving a car for my dad," David Oliver says. "We had built a new car and still had the old car. I suggested to my dad that Dale drive the old car. He was family."

The second generation of Earnhardt racers was about to begin.

3

The Web site choices seemed endless. There was Dave And Stacie's Page and NASCARICK'S Dale Earnhardt Page and Mr. Slick's Racing and Intmd8or and Tony's Dale Earnhardt Page and Hillbilly Hank's Tribute to NASCAR's Finest and Jim's Earnhardt Site and Frosty's Earnhardt Site and MAJIC3's Tribute To Dale and ... the list continued. The Internet was a place to speak and grieve, and much of the speaking and grieving was done in iambic pentameter.

A site that promised "Poems for Dale Earnhardt," played an instrumental version of Eric Clapton's "Tears in Heaven" in the background. A visitor could read poems entitled "A Hero in Our Hearts," "Kiss from T To 3," "A Poem for Dale Jr.," "No Ordinary Champion," "The Day Racing Died," "One Quarter Mile from Heaven," "One Last Start of the Engine," "Last Kiss," "The Man Who Drove the 3," "A Poem for No. 3,"

"The Final Turn," "The Intimidator," "Speedway in the Sky," "Gave My Life for My Son," "My Hero Is Gone," and many more.

A poem by peewee1966-DanaF was called "St. Earnhardt of Speed." It read:

A saint in Heaven is what you are
You ride a cloud, which is now your car
You cruise through Heaven with Style and Grace
As you did here with every race

The start of each race we think of you
Your Spirit and Light will guide us through
We ask of you on these special days
As we bow our heads and give you praise
You will move the angels through Heaven with glee
On your chariot, Cloud #3.

Our Hero, Our Saint, Dale Earnhardt of Speed.

A long-running Web site for the Fans Against Dale Earnhardt (FADE), built for people who hated the way he bullied and pushed his way to the front, showed only a message of sympathy to the Earnhardt family against a black screen.

GOING RACING

The car was a six-cylinder 1956 Ford Club Sedan. The Club Sedan part is important, because it meant the car had an aerodynamically inefficient post on the side at both doors. This was a vehicle that looked as if it had been built more for a nuclear family of four than for some aspiring Fireball Roberts. David Oliver had raced in it, OK, but it still needed something more to look like the terror on the racetrack that it surely would become with this new man behind the wheel.

The idea was that maybe a coat of paint would do the job.

"My cousins, Frank and Wayne, had a shop with a dyno machine," Gregg Dayvault says. "We'd done work for Ralph and David's father, Ray, putting their cars on the rollers for 'em, giving 'em the dyno tune. We all knew Dale and his brothers, Danny and Randy. We were all young'uns together.

"Helping Dale was just family helping family, the way it went. We had some paint around the shop. We just set about to painting the car."

The color choice was avocado. The roof already was purple with little gold metallic flecks in it. Avocado would be a fine color to go with the roof. Wayne mixed the paint. Wayne mixed wrong. The color came out pink.

"Dale Earnhardt drove a pink car in his first race," Wayne says. "That's a fact."

There would be marketing potential in future car designs—The Man in Black—but this was before markets and fame and advertising consultants. The Man in Pink was on the road.

The purple roof was painted pink to conform to the new color scheme. The words "Dayvault's Tune-Up & Brake Service" were painted in black on the back fenders. "K-2" was painted on the doors along with the word "Dale," written in script. The color maybe was wrong and the car maybe was wrong, but—check it out—the Russians hadn't been any more proud when they sent up Sputnik.

The race was at the old Concord Speedway, a cramped half-mile track that owner Henry Furr filled on Friday and Saturday nights with local folks looking to witness a little mayhem. The dust hung low every week—"You couldn't run that track today," Henry Furr says. "The EPA would be all over you"—and the passions ran high. Henry would try to straighten out all problems and had a couple of stitches in his head as evidence of his work.

"It sounds funny, but you could make more money running a track then than you can now," he says. "You'd pay $400 for a purse to win a race, charge $4 for people to get in, maybe run the whole show for $7,000. Dirt races last year . . . they had shows with a million dollars in purses. The tickets were $10, $15. The insurance alone will kill you. It was better back then. The cars were stronger, didn't fall apart as easy. The tires . . . you could drive up to Hickory and buy some recaps and run on them. It all was a lot more simple."

Furr had known Ralph for years. Furr would sponsor a Ford to run against Ralph and the other Chevys, because then "the Ford people and the Chevy people in the stands all would start fussin'." It was good for business. He'd known Dale for a long time, first as "this itty-bitty boy who'd come to the track with Ralph." Furr was interested when Dale took to the track for the first time.

"Back then, I guess you'd say he was like anybody else," Furr says. "But pretty soon you could see he was a natural."

There is no record of that first race on a dusty summer night. There certainly was no trophy. David Oliver drove the family's other car in the same race and doesn't remember lapping the new driver on the track, so the result couldn't have been too bad. ("He didn't get into no wrecks, I know that," he says.) Oliver does remember an impression he had, maybe from that race, maybe from the next few races.

"You could see that Dale knew what he was doing," David says. "He wasn't like someone just starting out. All the years with Ralph . . . he knew things that take other guys a lot of cars and a lot of time to learn. He knew when to make the move and when not to make the move, where the holes were. He knew things I didn't know.

"There was a thing that Ralph always said: 'You can't put it in you, but you can take it out of you.' It was about taking chances. You either could do that or not, either had that ability or not. And you could either use it or not."

The Man in Pink did not stay The Man in Pink very long. Oliver still drove the car sometimes, so there was no real schedule of races to run, no regularity, for a second driver. Earnhardt began looking for a next car to drive, a better situation. When he found it, he was gone. Oliver drove the pink car for a couple more years, actually won some races with it.

"I don't know what happened with it in the end," he says. "I know it's gone, crushed and recycled. Probably should have held on to it, huh? Be worth some money today."

Oliver stayed in racing and is a mechanic for the Roush racing team today. Frank and Wayne Dayvault moved to Myrtle Beach, but their cousin Gregg stayed in Kannapolis. He still is involved in cars, and one day, a couple of years ago, his son pointed out a beat-up '56 Club Sedan in back of the house. The son, Russ, now fifteen, had heard a lifetime of tales about the pink car. He suggested that he and his dad re-create it.

"And so we did," Gregg says. "Wayne, believe it or not, still remembered the formula he used for the paint. We matched it exactly. We put on all the same lettering. The car, I still have it, just looks slick. Too slick, in fact. It could really use some dents, some bruises.

"You know what I mean?"

The course was now set for the young Earnhardt for the next decade of struggle and hope. He was a race car driver. He could say that was what he was—"Hey, I raced at Concord the other night"—instead of just think about it. The daydream of childhood, looking out a classroom window, was a tangible, touchable reality. He was into the game, the process. The odd and dangerous game. The tangled process.

The problem was that there was no real ladder to climb toward success, no promotional scale from junior account executive to account executive on the way to the boardroom. The course was full of zigs and zags, ups and downs, a chart across a sheet of graph paper that would resemble a politician's popularity from crisis to crisis. The road to success went through a lot of blind and dark alleys. Banjo music played in the background.

All that mattered was racin'. Goin' racin'. He was married now, father of an infant son, Kerry, and that didn't matter. He soon would be divorced, and Kerry would be adopted by his ex-wife's second husband because the support checks didn't arrive. Racin'. Earnhardt would work jobs for money, money for racin'. The jobs would be no-future manual labor, in the weave room at the mill, under a car in a garage, putting up insulation, anything available, because they didn't matter. Racin' mattered. Where he lived, what he drove on the streets, how he dressed . . . nothing else was worth the bother.

Back in favor with his father, at last, he was sent by Ralph to the house of James Miller on the other side of town. James Miller was a race car owner. He had a junkyard behind his house that contained a couple of Ford Falcons that were available for duty as race cars. The Falcons were available because James Miller had been a race car driver, himself, until the previous year. That was when he had lost both his legs.

"I let another boy drive the car one night," he says. "I went along to work as his pit crew. I was washing off the windshield when a boy went out of control and mashed me into the front end. They took me to the hospital and took off both my legs. Walter Furr, no kin of Henry, made me some prosthetic legs."

Dale had been instructed to ask if he could drive one of the Falcons. He was working at the Great Dane Trucking Company as a welder on the 7 A.M. to 3 P.M. shift. He went to Miller's house with his request after work. Miller agreed to let him drive the car.

"You can drive it," James said. "If you do some work on it."

Dale began tearing at the car immediately. He was afraid that if he left and came back the next day, the offer would be taken back. He wound up working all night, then going straight to Great Dane Trucking. He returned to James Miller's house after work again the next night. Racin'. He had a race car to drive.

"We eventually took it down to Concord," James says. "Dale was good, but we wore out that car that first year. He crashed everywhere. He was just trying things, seeing what he could do. He'd see a hole and think he could make it through, and sometimes he could, but sometimes he couldn't. Ralph would talk with him, teach him what to do.

"The next year, I built a new garage and we built a new car. That car was better. And Dale didn't crash as much."

Ralph became involved in building the new car, another '56 Falcon. He set up the car, working a lot with James. James would spend long days with Ralph in the garage, some days talking about everything in the world, other days when Ralph would grunt and say nothing. James never could figure it out. Ralph was Ralph. The car turned out to be pretty good.

"I was there when Dale won his first race at Concord Speedway," James Miller says. "Ralph was there, too. Dale won a few races that year. Did good. The next year, I sold the car to the Russell brothers in Concord. Dale went with them."

The move turned out to be very good for Dale. The Russell brothers had another car, a better car to drive. In his first year with them he won 17 races. The next year he won 36. He won nine straight at one time at Metrolina Fairgrounds Speedway, so many that the promoters put a bounty on his head. This was the kind of stuff that happened to Ralph. The son was showing signs he could drive like the father. He also still was crashing.

"The Russell brothers' garage was across the street from my business," Dink Widenhouse says. "I'd stop in sometimes. One day I stopped in and Dale was there. He'd rolled the car good a couple nights earlier, and now they were fixing it. While they were doing it, they were looking for ways to take off some weight, to make it faster."

Widenhouse noticed that the car had an airplane battery. An airplane battery was different from a car battery because it had lead balls inside. When the airplane turned upside down, the lead balls would lock into place and keep the water from spilling out of the battery. The lead balls weighed, total, maybe a pound.

"You know, that's an airplane battery you have there," Widenhouse said to the Russell brothers. "If you took out those lead balls, you could probably save a pound right away. . . ."

He looked at Earnhardt.

"Nah," Widenhouse said. "You better leave those lead balls in there."

———————

Earnhardt was working now at Punch's Wheel Alignment Service on Route 29 in Concord. This was another of the no-future jobs, a lot of grease and dirt, a time clock to whack every morning. The bays were in a low, wooden building down a small hill from the main office on the road where Punch sold custom chrome wheels and tires to the hotrod kids of the area.

The business still exists, although wheel alignments no longer are done. The low building—the words PUNCH'S WHEEL ALIGNMENT. MONRO-MATIC SHOCKS SOLD HERE still visible in chipped and faded tiles on the roof—mostly is used for storage.

"The roof is unbelievable," Punchy Whitaker, the late Punch's son, now in charge, says. "If you bought a sign, there's not a chance in the world it would last for forty years. But here's that roof. Just won't quit. People still pull in here and want a wheel alignment. The roof keeps going."

Punchy . . .

(OK, a word about southern nicknames. Humpy Wheeler, the president of Lowe's Speedway, is named Humpy after his dad, who was a football player at the University of Illinois with Red Grange. The dad was caught smoking one day by the coach. The dad's brand of choice was Camels. After the obligatory punishment, the coach began referring to the dad as "Humpy." The name stuck and was handed down to the next Humpy in the family.

(Punch Whitaker was nicknamed for the way he hit a baseball, sort of punched it through the hole for singles. His son, Donald, became "Little Punch" or "Punchy." The problem was he also had another son, Howard, who also was nicknamed "Little Punch" and "Punchy." This was confusing until Howard moved out of Concord for a large part of his adult life. Donald had full rights to the name. Howard, alas, has returned to the area. Donald told him it would be fine to return, but the name was gone. "You're just going to have to be Howard," Punchy said.)

Punchy remembers Earnhardt as "pretty headstrong. I don't guess 'cocky' was the right word, but it came close." He remembers giving the keys to a late-model Corvette to Earnhardt one day. The Whitakers owned another building on the other side of the highway, which is divided by a grass strip. The Corvette was at the other building and needed some kind of work in the shop. Earnhardt was supposed to drive to the U-turn, come back on the other side, and deliver the Corvette to the shop. He made the chore a challenge.

"He leaves the parking lot, wide open," Punchy says. "He screams around the U-turn. He comes back, wide open, skids to a stop. I go running across the highway, almost get myself killed, to see what the heck he was doing. He looks at me with that smile and says, 'Runs good.'"

Punchy keeps a framed copy of a canceled Earnhardt paycheck in the cramped office. ("We probably got a bunch more of them, too, somewhere," he says.) The check is from October 13, 1973. The signature is a more basic version of the autograph that became trademarked and famous. The amount is $202.41. Wheel-alignment specialists were paid every two weeks.

"Doesn't seem like much, does it?" Punchy says. "Then, again 1973, everything doesn't seem like much."

Two important events happened at Punch's Wheel Alignment Service. The first was that Earnhardt eventually quit. No one is sure of the exact date, but he left with the pronouncement that he was "going to become a full-time race car driver." The elder Punch gave the immortal, misguided reply, "You're going to starve, boy." ("My daddy would have been right 999 out of 1,000 times," Punchy says. "But I guess he kinda blew that one.") The second important event was that on September 26, 1973, seventeen days before Punch issued that check in the frame, a woman came to the shop to tell Earnhardt that his father was sick and in the hospital. The reality was much more serious than that.

A heart attack had killed Ralph Earnhardt at the age of forty-five.

The scene has been made more dramatic in countless Earnhardt stories and biographies, and Hollywood no doubt will take the dramatic approach, too, the auto-racing son coming into the garage to find his father dead over an open engine or the auto-racing son working on a carburetor with his father at the moment of the attack, but the truth was everyday sad and normal. Ralph died on the kitchen floor. Martha found him.

He had suffered an unnoticed attack earlier in the year that was discovered only when he went to the hospital complaining of discomfort in his throat and chest. The doctors had put him on medication and advised him to stay out of his car for a while. Ralph complied, but returned to the Sportsman wars when he felt better near the end of the summer.

His death was an understandable shock to his oldest son. After their estrangement when Dale quit school, the two men had come back together. Dale always thought that when he managed a Sunoco station when he was eighteen for a couple of weeks, eighty hours a week, after the owner died, the freeze would begin to lift. His father, perhaps, saw some signs of a future in him. Whatever. Maybe it simply was time, the natural progression of relationships between fathers and sons.

They had a driving bond now. They didn't compete in races, Dale mostly driving semi-modifieds, Ralph in the Sportsman, but they often raced on the same track on the same night in different events. They talked cars. They worked on cars. Ralph's lifelong lessons had also moved to the laboratory.

"I'd see him showing Dale things at the old Concord dirt track," Freddie Smith, who still drives dirt cars, says. "There'd be times set up at the track for practice. Ralph would be in one car, Dale in another. Ralph would be pushing him deep into the corners from behind, showing him what to do."

The one time the two men drove in the same race became one of Dale's favorite stories. He told it everywhere in later years, his own little stock-car parable. The tale contained all the elements that he associated with his father: skill, craftiness, great guidance, inspiration . . . and love.

The race was at the Metrolina Speedway outside Charlotte. A scheduling conflict had diluted the Sportsman field, half the drivers going to another track. The promoters needed to fill out the starting lineup, so they announced that the top five finishers in the semi-modifieds, Dale's class, would be allowed to enter the Sportsman race.

Dale finished second in the semi-modifieds behind some driver, name forgotten, he couldn't pass. The guy's car simply was stronger. Nevertheless, Dale was in the Sportsman field. So was the other guy.

"So we're running in the Sportsman race," Dale would say. "It's late in the race. Daddy's leading. Another Sportsman car is second. The other guy in the semi-modifieds is third. I'm fourth. I still can't get by the guy. He's too fast. With a few laps to go, I see Daddy come up behind me. He's lapping me. I move over to let him pass, but Daddy moves with me. He comes up on my bumper! He starts pushing me! He pushes me past the other guy! Daddy wins! I finish third. The other guy, fourth, is so mad, complaining everywhere about 'those Earnhardts,' but there's nothing he can do. It's over."

The ending to the story always would be wistful, either spoken or unspoken. What if Daddy hadn't died? What if this sort of stuff had continued, a partnership in all that future success? If Ralph had only lived until he was fifty-one, he would have seen his son become Rookie of the Year and then a Winston Cup champion. If he'd lived until sixty-five, he would seen all seven Winston Cup championships. If he were still alive, he would have been only seventy-one this year at Daytona . . . what if he could have seen it all? Wouldn't that have been the biggest kick there was?

"Daddy was honest, quiet, and independent," Dale said in a 1986 interview with Tom Higgins of the *Charlotte Observer.* "I think it was his independence that maybe was the reason he didn't go much further in racing. Lord knows he had the know-how to go on. I stood on his tow truck as a boy, and I think I must have seen every lap he ever drove. I guess you would say I adopted his style of driving and I try to capitalize on what he told me, all the advice he gave me. I wish I'd paid more attention.

"It has been a long time, but he's still an everyday thought. Whenever I have a problem, inside the race car or out, I still think, 'How would he have handled this situation? What would he have done?' He's still a big part of me."

There should have been more. That was the final line about Ralph. Even though he was the Sportsman champion in 1956 and was elected to the NASCAR Hall of Fame, he basically was a local hero. He never caught the big break. He never forced the big break. He raced against the biggest names—the Pettys and Fireball Roberts and David Pearson and the Flock brothers and Junior Johnson—and sometimes beat them, but never in the biggest places. He was a master of the minor leagues, local legend, consigned to the memories of only the biggest fans, wrapped up in the question "Yeah, those other guys are good, but did you ever see Ralph Earnhardt drive?" He never broke out of the garage on Sedan Avenue.

"Ralph's timing was off in his life span, that was his biggest problem," onetime Sportsman driver Tommy Houston says. "He never did get the big break, the big ride. He'd win so many races the promoters would get mad because he was keeping fans away . . . but he did it all too early."

"We went to some Winston Cup races, but Ralph didn't like 'em," Uncle Dub says. "There was too much traveling involved. He wanted to be home. I'll tell you this, he absolutely wouldn't have been able to deal with the NASCAR of today. He hated politics. I remember, we'd go to Columbia on Thursday nights. The promoter ran there on Thursdays because he didn't want to buck high school football, which was very big on Friday nights in South Carolina. Well, every once in a while, there'd be a rainout and the race would be postponed until Friday. The promoter would be pleading with Ralph to hang around. He'd offer dinner, hotel room, the whole thing. Nope, Ralph wouldn't take it. He'd rather drive all the way home and come all the way back than owe the promoter something. That's the way he was."

He was buried at Center Grove Lutheran cemetery in Kannapolis. His headstone was a bit different from most. A race car, the No. 8 on the side, was carved next to the usual information. The grave has become much more busy since Dale's death, a place for mourners to go, but always has had a certain attraction.

"My accountant lives right across the street from Martha," Dink Widenhouse says. "I had to go there one day a couple of years ago with a man from the IRS. He was checking all the books in my business. I was scared to death.

"We were at the accountant's all day. This IRS man looked at everything. Didn't say much. When we came out, just to make small talk, I said, 'Did you ever hear of Ralph Earnhardt? The racer? Dale's father?'

The IRS man said he had. He seemed impressed. I said, 'That's his house right over there. That's his garage in the back. I used to race against him. Want to take a look?' We went back and looked at the garage, and then I said, 'He's buried right near here. Want to see his grave?' The IRS man wanted to see that, too. We went out to the grave, saw the little car on the headstone, said a prayer, and left. Finally, on the way back to the office, I had the courage to ask, 'How's everything look?' The IRS man said, 'You're OK.' Just like that.

"I've got to tell Martha . . . all these years later, Ralph Earnhardt was still able to help me out."

———————

The restraints were lifted after Ralph was gone. That probably was the biggest change in Dale Earnhardt's life, both pro and con. Would his route have been easier with Ralph's knowledge of the racing scene, with Ralph's guidance, his ability to open doors easier? Maybe so. Would Ralph's conservative approach have been a muffler, stifling a son's all-costs enthusiasm, a constant word of caution? Also, maybe so. The debate really didn't matter. Ralph was gone now. There was no word of caution. None that the son could hear.

He sold off Ralph's favorite two hunting dogs, dealt with his grief, and roared into his chosen profession the same way he approached a race. Go to the front. Go as fast as you can. Consequences be damned. Ralph's bottom-line economics, counting every nut and bolt and dollar bill, knowing that every ding on a fender cost money, was the exact opposite of his son's style. Ralph had never been hurt seriously in a race car, a broken foot his biggest injury. He was not a man to take big chances. His son was a different matter. Dale acted like he never even thought about the risk.

"People take out loans to buy a house and, in the end, they get a house," he once said. "I took out loans to race. In the end, I got racin'."

He ran up bills wherever he could, hoping to win enough money to pay them later. Loans? He took loans in the spring that he hoped he could repay in the fall after the races were done. He stretched himself as far as he could and then stretched himself even farther. Choosing between a needed radiator hose and a sandwich, the radiator hose always won.

He was married again, this time to Brenda Gee, the daughter of garage owner Robert Gee, and they had a daughter, Kelley, born on August 28, 1972, and then a son, Dale Jr., born on October 10, 1974. They lived in a succession of apartments and trailers before winding up in a double-wide parked behind the old family house on Sedan Avenue. Dale wound up reopening Ralph's garage, building a canopy outside and working on his cars out there.

He would reflect often in later, more quiet times about this period of his life when there was a question about whether he was chasing his dream or chasing his tail:

"We probably should have been on welfare," he said in a *Sports Illustrated* article in 1995. "Racing cost me my second marriage for the things I took away from my family. For our family cars, we drove old junk Chevelles, anything we could get for $200."

Racing was the priority. There always was something that had broken in one race that had to be fixed for the next race. There always was money that had to be found. David Oliver remembers Saturday mornings at the three auto parts stores in Kannapolis at the time—Ralph Deal's, the NAPA store, and Sam Stroup's store. Racers would arrive early, looking to replace the part that had failed in Friday night's race so their cars would be ready for Saturday night's race. Earnhardt was part of the crowd. Sometimes.

"Dale Earnhardt did business with us, but not a lot of business," Sam Stroup's son, running the shop now, says. "Because he didn't pay his bills. He was too busy running around and hunting and fishing to pay his bills."

He was like a million other guys in their early twenties, then and now, too young for the responsibility and commitment that had landed on them so fast, refusing to accept it, grabbing for a freedom they thought they should own but already had squandered. Young and dumb. Earnhardt once used that term himself. The taverns are full of these guys every Friday night in every town in America.

This guy was in a race car. That was the only difference. He was as testosterone crazy as the rest of them, except he was drunk with danger.

"He's the only guy I knew from back then who became what he said he wanted to be," Marshall Brooks, a friend from that time, says. "That's why it cost him two wives."

Brooks, who now runs a used-car lot and is also a preacher in a small Baptist church, talks about taking a ride with Earnhardt one night in a brand-new El Camino truck. Earnhardt had kept the truck overnight from wherever he was working. The truck, remember, was not his.

"We're driving on this back road and he does this 360 with it," Brooks says. "Then he does another one. Two 360s in a row. Then we're going about 80 down this long hill and we just bottomed out at the end. Thump. There were two little dents in the roof where we hit our heads."

Brooks was racing motorcycles at the time and running "Doc's Cycle Center" and was involved a little bit in the cannabis trade. He was living his own version of the flat-out life. He would pay Earnhardt $75 a week to put the name of the motorcycle shop on the race car. He would help out with payments for tires and parts.

One night he and Earnhardt were driving in the truck Brooks used to haul his motorcyles. The truck had a loudspeaker built into the sound system. Earnhardt said they should play a trick on his brother-in-law. He directed Brooks to the designated address, where they parked the truck and announced, through the loudspeaker, that the place was surrounded and everyone should come out with their hands up.

Alas, there was no reaction, so Brooks took Earnhardt home. As he took himself home, he suddenly saw the blue lights of four squad cars in the back window. Uh-oh. The house didn't belong to Earnhardt's brother-in-law, but to Cliff Cook, his boyhood friend from Car Town, who now was a cop. Cook had called other cops. Brooks had to talk his way out of trouble.

"I'm there and I have a sawed-off shotgun and who-knows-what in the truck," Brooks says. "I get out of it, though, and Dale just laughed the next day. He thought it was the funniest thing in the world."

Brooks's own tour of the wild side ended with his choice to become a preacher. (He says in later days his congregation once helped Dale's second wife, Brenda, move from the projects with her two children and get into a house.) He found the Lord through dramatic circumstances.

Tending bar one night in a small tavern, he witnessed a man pull a gun and shoot two people, neither fatally. Brooks had a gun behind the bar and shot at the shooter as the shooter exited. He thought he had missed, hitting the frame of the door, but police later found the man, bleeding, not far from the bar. When the man somehow escaped jail time, Brooks became terrified. He decided the man was going to kill him. There seemed to be only one response.

"I decided I had to kill him first," he says. "I had it all planned. He lived in a trailer. I had a hand grenade. I was going to open the door and throw in the grenade."

He had driven by the trailer a number of times, plotting his moves, before he realized how paranoid he had become. What was he doing? Was he crazy? This was his first step toward religion.

"I just looked at myself," Marshall Brooks says in his used-car office, a shotgun and pistol still in plain sight in case trouble might arrive. "I was thinking about killing someone. How could I do that? The guy's trailer, in fact, was just around the corner from Dale's mother's house."

Earnhardt made the full-time switch from dirt to asphalt racing in that troubled year, 1974. He bought a used race car from Harry Gant, an established racer in Taylorsville, and worked on it himself and attacked the Sportsman division of NASCAR racing. The Sportsman division now is the Busch circuit, a high-profile stepping-stone to the Winston Cup, races often held on Saturday at the same track where the Cup race would be held on Sunday. The cars and costs are similar to the cars and costs in Winston Cup.

This was not the case in 1974. The Sportsman division was almost as formless and unruly as the dirt car circuit. This was not AAA baseball, do well and be called up to the big club. There was AAA baseball in a lot of places, and the big club wasn't so big anyway.

"The Sportsman division was so disorganized, so messed up, it just existed by itself," racing historian Gene Granger says. "They had standings, but there were a lot of standings. This wasn't a national thing. It was regional. If you raced in New England, you raced one circuit. If you raced in the Southwest, you raced another. If you raced around here, you raced Sportsman. That was important for Dale. If he had grown up in some other part of the country, I don't know if we'd ever have seen Dale Earnhardt. It's not like today, where drivers come from anywhere."

There were a lot of drivers who never bothered moving out of Sportsman. A living could be made on this backup string of shows. Why fight the two and three powerful teams in Winston Cup? You could work a modest budget and actually win in Sportsman. This was a more manageable horizon. A driver named L. D. Ottinger kept a real job in a manufacturing plant and still won championships in 1975 and '76. Ralph Earnhardt won in '56. Harry Gant won. Jack Ingram won. Tommy Houston won a lot. He won 24 races and wound up with 417 career starts, a Busch record, between 1982 and 1996.

"I was a little older, so I started racing about five years before Dale," Houston says. "I got to run against his father for two or three years. It was pretty basic back then. The cars weren't anything like today. You could get an old frame out of a scrap yard, check to see if it wasn't bent, then build a race car on top of it. Your friends would work on it with you. You'd drive it. Very few people back then raced full-time."

Houston was from Hickory, North Carolina. His father was a house-painter, never involved in racing, but Tommy had three older brothers who were drawn to the sport by the little dirt track in town. The oldest, Hal, came out of the service, worked in a furniture plant during the week, and drove on the weekends. He handed the sport down.

"My brother Ken raced with him," Tommy says. "They were terrors on the dirt. They raced against Tiny Lund, Bud Moore, all of them. Hal wound up quitting when he had a family and just didn't have the money that it took to keep a car going."

Houston remembers Earnhardt coming along, "Ralph's kid," another hard charger added to the scene. They got along, became friendly. They were doing the same things, hitting the same stops. Ralph's kid could drive you crazy, but you never could stay mad at him.

"That's the thing," Houston says. "He'd do some terrible things to you on the track, but then he'd be your friend. He'd come over and say, 'Hey, don't be mad at me. Don't stay mad. You're mad? Do the same thing to me next week.' He broke four of my ribs on the left side once—this was later—at Indianapolis Raceway Park. Carried me inside on turn four, carried me inside until I had no place to go and I crashed. Four ribs. 'Don't be mad at me,' he said. And, for some reason, you weren't."

There seemed to be races everywhere, so many that a driver could pick and choose where he'd have his best shot. There was Savannah, Georgia, on Thursday nights; a choice between Asheville and Richmond on Friday; South Boston, Virginia, or Hickory or Myrtle Beach on Saturday; Merriville, Tennessee, on Sunday. The driving to and from the races was more demanding than the driving at the races. Everything would be done with one car, hitched to the back of a truck. Home late every night. On the road every day. Sleep was Monday and Tuesday.

Houston remembers racing against Earnhardt through the mountains every time they would go to Bristol. This was a four-hour drive from Charlotte. The road, U.S. Route 421, bends and turns and has all those signs, "Truckers Check Your Brakes," and gravel turnoffs for out-of-control tractor-trailers. Houston would be towing his car with a '57 Chevy truck. Earnhardt would be towing with his father's truck. It would be a race, the trucks and cars bouncing and banging and clanging, as two maniacs drove as fast as they could. It would be a hoot.

"We'd get to the end, stop for a sandwich, get fuel," Houston says. "Laugh at each other."

Earnhardt was driven to succeed, to make it, whatever "it" was. He was traveling the rounds of the local garages, looking for a better ride, looking for help. ("I loaned him $50 the first time he ever raced at Darlington," Henry Furr, the owner of the Concord track, says. "Did I get it back? He was a race car driver. You don't loan money to race car drivers thinking you're going to get it back.") Houston was more settled. He liked what he was doing. He liked life as it was.

"It was just so much fun to race against people, to beat them and win," he says. "It was all so basic. You know all that talk about the seat belt and safety equipment now? You had a lap belt back then. No shoulder harness, not at the start. I remember the seat belt didn't fit once. I just cut it myself and put it back together with quarter-inch bolts. That's what you did. Who knew?"

He says he has a picture of Earnhardt's car from those days. It is a car that Robert Gee owned, orange and white. It has been involved in a crash. All four tires have been knocked off. They're scattered across the ground. Earnhardt has crawled out of the car.

"I showed it to him once," Houston says. "I said, 'You recognize this?'"

The biggest connection between Houston and Earnhardt turned out to be an introduction. Houston's brother Hal, the first racer in the family, would come to some of Tommy's races with his family. Hal had a daughter. When she didn't come to the races with her parents, she came with her girlfriends.

"She was pretty," Tommy Houston says. "She was bright, too. She had finished all of her courses in high school by the end of her junior year, so they just let her graduate with the seniors. Then I think she even did a couple years of college."

Teresa Houston was sixteen years old when she met Dale Earnhardt. More, much more, would follow.

"And I guess it's because of me," Tommy Houston says, retired now from the wars, with one son, Andy, driving in Winston Cup and a second son, Marty, driving in the Busch series.

Earnhardt's debut in Winston Cup competition came on Memorial Day in 1975 at the Charlotte Motor Speedway in the Charlotte 600. One of the stops on his perpetual garage tour for parts/help/conversation belonged to an owner/driver in Concord named Ed Negre. Negre had a newer, better car for the race, and his son, Norman, suggested he also enter the old car and let this kid Earnhardt, who always was around, drive it.

Norman was not being totally charitable. Norman wanted to be the crew chief for the race.

"You kids'll never qualify it," Negre said about the car.

"Well, give us a chance," his son said. "Dale's going to be a great driver."

Negre was skeptical, but he went with Norman to watch a Sportsman race at Metrolina to check out Earnhardt's abilities. Flying to the front at the start, Earnhardt took the early lead. Norman had a told-you-so smile. He pointed out Earnhardt's success to his dad.

"Yeah, he's good," Ed agreed. "But you know what, Norman? All these young guys are good. They're the same. All good."

Then funny things happened. Ed isn't sure what the sequence was and what the actual events were, but Earnhardt ran into trouble a couple of times. Maybe a blown tire. Maybe something under the hood. At any rate, Earnhardt wound up losing his lead and going back to the pits. Ed wrote him off and kept watching the race. Oops, here was Earnhardt again, back at the front. How'd he do that? Oops, there he was, back in the pits. Told you so. Oops, here he was, back in front. How'd he do that? After about the third return to the lead, Ed turned to his son.

"You know what, Norman?" he said. "You're right. This guy can drive."

Norman, indeed, was made the crew chief for the old car for the Charlotte 600. Earnhardt was made the driver. Winston Cup was still young—Winston had come into the game only four years earlier as a sponsor, the "modern," shortened schedule of 31 races, down from 48, established only three years earlier—and the drivers and owners very much were operating on a caste system. There were the three or four big-money teams on the circuit like the Wood brothers and the Pettys and Junior Johnson, and they were the only ones who really had a chance to win the race. Everybody else was filling out the field and jostling for position.

"It was almost like there was a race within a race for the rest of us," Negre says. "You'd be lucky to finish in the top ten. It really wasn't that expensive to race at that time. You could build yourself a decent car for $20,000. You'd go out there and keep track of how many laps everybody was down on the leaders, go from there. Hope that people would fall out, that something would happen to everyone else."

Negre tried to impress Earnhardt with these realities before the race. Negre's car was a Dodge. He told Earnhardt that a Dodge certainly was not going to win. A famous name was going to win. OK? The plan for the day was to run cautiously and smart, to have fun and finish. OK? There was one other thing: This was a 600-mile race. Earnhardt never had driven a race even half as long. The key to this kind of race was to relax. This would be a hot, long day. The crew would pack a three-gallon jug of water in the car hooked to a tube that would serve as a straw. Stay cool.

The two drivers climbed into their Dodges and rolled into action. Earnhardt started 33rd. Negre tried to keep track of him.

About a third of the way into the race, Negre noticed Earnhardt was in the pits. He wondered what was wrong. This was an unscheduled stop. Using the one two-way radio he owned, he called the pits.

"What's wrong with Dale?" he asked.

"Nothing" was the reply.

"No, what's wrong with Dale?"

"Nothing."

"Look, what's wrong?"

"Nothing" was the reply again. "He just come in for a drink of water. He was thirsty."

Thirsty?

"I used that against him for the rest of his career," Negre says. "The last time I saw him, in fact, was out in California. I walked up and said, 'Dale, where do you want me to wait with a big bucket of water?' He just laughed. He drank three gallons of water in one-third of the race. Do you believe it?"

Earnhardt finished 22nd, a first Winston Cup purse of $2,425. He got to keep 40 percent of it. Negre finished 24th. The driver in between, at 23rd, was another low-buget driver/owner named Richard Childress.

"I would have liked to have kept two cars in Winston Cup, but I just didn't have the money, so that was the only time Dale drove for me," Negre says. "I tried to keep him around for the next season, tried to work a deal with Richard Howard, the owner at Charlotte, to get a Petty engine, get something going, but Richard Howard said he didn't want any part of it. He said about Dale, 'No, he ain't nobody.' I said, 'Yes he is. He's going to be a superstar.'

"About three or four years later, I read a quote from Richard Howard that said just about the same thing I said. It made me mad. I was just a little guy, though, and didn't have the money to back him. One more time it shows that you gotta have money to make money."

Negre, in fact, soon was out of the business. ("It got too expensive," he says. "I was a West Coast guy, anyway, so I went back to the state of Washington and bought me a logging truck.") Norman tried to keep the race team going, but drifted into car building for other people. One of the things he did when he disbanded the operation was sell the number on the car. The number was 8.

"So the first race Dale Earnhardt ever drove in Winston Cup was No. 8, my number, same number as his dad," Ed Negre says. "Then, a few years ago, he bought the number, himself, and gave it to his son. No. 8. I see his son drive and I say, 'That's Ralph's number and Dale Jr.'s number and that's my number.'"

4

AT THE ALTAR

The plan for the Bennett Funeral Home on 209 East Main Street in Concord, New Hampshire, at the other end of the country from Daytona, Florida, simply was to put out a book for people to sign in memory of Dale Earnhardt. This was something the directors had done in the past when famous people died. The last occasion was the death of Princess Diana.

"It's a way for people to deal with their grief," general manager Nick Sousi says. "We put an ad in the paper and say this is taking place, sort of an 'open house.' People can leave their messages and we send the books along to the family involved. People somehow feel better afterwards."

This open house became a bit more elaborate. The simple memorial moment grew and grew.

A number of collectors of memorabilia brought in their collections to be on display. The wife of a security guard made little black ribbons with the number 3 on the front to hand to every visitor. A Goodyear dealer supplied some racing slicks. The local Chevy dealer supplied some lithographs. An altar was constructed with a picture of Earnhardt in the middle, flanked by two large floral bouquets. A number of beer and cigarette signs—WELCOME RACE FANS!—were hung on the chapel walls.

"The room, I must admit, looked a lot like a bar by the time we got done," Sousi says.

The crowd started coming. Visiting hours were from 10 A.M. to 4 P.M. on Saturday, February 24. The first visitor arrived at 7:30 A.M.

"We told the woman that we didn't open until ten, so she should just go and have breakfast and come back," Sousi says. "She said, 'I've already had breakfast, thank you.' And she just waited in the parking lot."

Sousi estimated the line at 200 when the chapel opened. The people kept coming. He says they filled a number of books with messages. The final total of signatures was "over 1,500."

"It'll be the biggest service we'll have this year," Sousi says. "No doubt."

MAKING IT

The hardest part of driving a race car fast is finding someone to furnish the fast race car. That always had been the story. A line of drivers that started well before Ralph Earnhardt and goes well into today is filled with talented and brave men—and the occasional woman—who went through entire careers, good careers, without ever having a chance to drive good equipment.

If a jockey's success is tied to the quality of horses he rides, a race car driver is even more influenced by the quality of cars he drives. A lowly bred thoroughbred champion sometimes arrives on the scene, a Seattle Slew, that rushes to a Triple Crown despite the odds and brings the little man on top along with him. There are no Seattle Slews in auto racing. Form is followed much more closely. A big-time race car is built with big-time money.

A driver needs a backer with big-time money.

"Driving a stock car on the small tracks and in the small races is like singing in a Holiday Inn lounge," someone once suggested to Freddie Smith, the dirt car driver. "You go out there, do the best you can every night, but you need that big agent to come through the door and sign you to the contract. No matter how well you sing, you'll go nowhere until the guy shows up."

"Yeah, you're at the Holiday Inn," Freddie Smith replied. "You're waiting, but most times they don't find your room. They never found mine."

The wait for Dale Earnhardt seemed endless. The one-shot, thirsty ride at the Charlotte 600 was just that, a one-shot, thirsty ride that left him still as an "ain't nobody." He was still bumping around garages, still driving his own Sportsman car, still scuffling, looking for sponsors, for a better ride, for the big chance. He was moving from apartment to apartment to trailer home. His second marriage was going, going, eventually gone in 1977 with the stress of it all. The creditors were calling. He was back in his mother's house, living in the trailer in the backyard.

There were a few more shots at Winston Cup, two in '76, one more in '77, but they were the same as the ride with Ed Negre. "Strokin'" was the term. Get out there in inferior equipment. Do the best you can.

Understand you have no chance to win. The second ride in '76 was the only one most people remembered. And that was for the wrong reasons.

"I'd crashed at Daytona and got hurt," Johnny Ray, a former owner/driver from Eastaboga, Alabama, says. "They took the car to Robert Gee's shop in Concord to get fixed. The car was fixed pretty soon, but I wasn't. I knew Dale from hanging around the shop. He wanted to drive the car at Atlanta. It seemed like a good idea. I wasn't going to drive."

The good idea turned bad on lap 271 of a 328-lap race, the Dixie 500. The steering on driver Dick Brooks's car failed. Earnhardt, following directly behind Brooks, hit the car squarely and went flying. He flipped "four or five times . . . the scariest accident in the superspeedway's 17-year history," according to the *Charlotte Observer.* He walked away with a slightly cut hand.

"He would have driven more for me, he was doing good before the crash, but that was my only car," Johnny Ray says. "I was out of business and he was out of business."

Earnhardt had become so frustrated at his lack of progress, he'd gone back to dirt cars. Enough was enough. He was driving for Robert Gee, his father-in-law, even as the marriage fell apart and then died, winning a bunch of dirt races just to win races and to try to pay bills. He was test-driving a Chrysler product called the Kit Car for veteran crew chief Harry Hyde, a sort of do-it-yourself race car kit. He was floundering. He was thinking about selling some of his racing equipment to pay bills.

Even when he lucked into a five-race ride for Winston Cup in 1978, replacing African-American driver Willy T. Ribbs at the last moment, after Ribbs didn't show up for practice and was cited for a traffic violation for driving the wrong way down a one-way street a few days before the first race, it was a no-future assignment. Will Cronkite, the team owner, was a good engine builder but didn't have the big money. Earnhardt was strokin' again.

Would it never end? What did he have to do? He was getting older now. Was he going to be in the long line of close-but-never-beens with his father? What? Time was running out on him. He had passed his twenty-seventh birthday. He still needed the big break.

He had no idea the wheels had begun to spin already.

———————

"My middle daughter was going out with this boy who drove at the Santa Clara County Fairgrounds on Saturday nights," California businessman Rod Osterlund, now retired at Lake Tahoe, says. "I wound up helping him a little bit, sponsoring the car, things like that. I'd never been involved in racing, except maybe a little drag racing as a kid, but I wound up going. It was a good time and so forth.

"I also wound up helping out another driver, Roland Wlodyka. That went on for a while, and then my daughter's boyfriend stopped driving and then stopped being my daughter's boyfriend and I probably would have been out of racing. Except I still had Roland."

This all was happening around the same time in 1975 when Earnhardt was making that first ride in the Winston Cup at Charlotte. Osterlund was a builder and developer of real estate on the West Coast. He sponsored Wlodyka, after the boyfriend left, for another season in sprint cars and, surprise, saw a return on his investment. Needing a place to diversify his income, Osterlund decided this might be a good and fun possibility. He talked with Wlodyka about options for further involvement. Wlodyka talked about the racing "back east." He meant Winston Cup, NASCAR.

"Let's check it out," Osterlund said.

He sent Wlodyka on a fact-finding mission, and the report back was encouraging. Winston Cup very much seemed to be an area that could be attacked with a new approach, new thinking. The big motor companies, Ford and GM and Chrysler, had dropped the direct sponsorship deals that had allowed two or three race teams to have complete control over the sport. Any owner now could have the same access to racing equipment, over the counter, that only the big teams previously had from the research and development department. The door for success was open to someone new who was willing to invest substantial amounts of money . . . and not a lot of people were coming through the door.

Osterlund went to some Winston Cup races, studied the Petty operation at Level Cross, North Carolina, and talked with legend Junior Johnson. He picked stock car brains wherever he could. The idea seemed better and better. It made business sense. Osterlund decided Winston Cup "smelled good."

"In 1977, we went to Michigan in the middle of the year for our first race, with Roland driving the car," he says. "That was our plan, to have Roland drive. It turned out, though, that Roland wasn't really good at it. He was a good sprint car driver, but he was too old to start something new, didn't have the knack of driving a stock car. There was one time . . . someone heard this on the radio during the middle of a race at Bristol . . . Richard Petty said, 'That Roland from Poland is going to kill us if he doesn't get out of here.'"

Osterlund nevertheless wound up staying with the sport, but with a different driver, Dave Marcis, for the 1978 season. Roland wound up staying, heading the operation, which was set up in a modern garage in Derita, outside Charlotte. Osterlund became a commuter, taking care of his real business in California and his new business in North Carolina.

He jumped into the chase. He hired top mechanics. He brought in top equipment, cars built from the bottom up. He gave his people health coverage and benefits. He gave bonuses on performance and for Christmas. No one had done this in NASCAR on this scale. Roland fabricated a hauler, a trailer, that could carry two cars to a race at one time. The old NASCAR hands stared in half derision, half wonder. No one had done this. Osterlund was looking at the old southern game with new, bottom-line, California eyes.

"We approached the sport from the beginning with the goal of winning the championship," Osterlund says. "We weren't stroking. The strokers made the show, bless 'em, for all those years, but we didn't want that. We wanted to win. Ask Dave Marcis today, and I'll bet he'll tell you that the car he drove that year was one of the best rides he ever had."

When the '78 season unfolded, with all of this attention and hope, Osterlund and Wlodyka quickly decided they had made one major miscalculation. They didn't like their choice of driver. They didn't think Marcis was testing the car in races enough. They felt he was solid, a fine guy, certainly competent, stayed away from trouble, finished most of the time in a respectable third or fourth or fifth . . . but he never won. He didn't take the chances they wanted.

Osterlund and Wlodyka, impatient, began looking for a different driver. They didn't have to look far. Of course.

"Dale came around the shop all the time," Wlodyka says. "We gave him used parts. So I knew him pretty well."

The idea was to have someone drive a second Osterlund car, the No. 98 car, in the final race of the year in Atlanta. The car was a rebuilt Monte Carlo that had been wrecked by Benny Parsons. Putting it into the race would give the team a two-car entry, also something that was new at the time. If it worked out, perhaps the team would run two drivers for the entire '79 season.

Wlodyka campaigned for Earnhardt as the driver. That made Osterlund interested. Humpy Wheeler, who had become a friend, also campaigned for Earnhardt. That made Osterlund doubly interested. Humpy offered Osterlund $5,000 if he put Earnhardt in the car. That clinched the deal.

"There's a lot of stories about how Dale Earnhardt's success began," Osterlund says. "The real story is that Humpy gave me $5,000. I was in business. Five thousand dollars was not an insignificant amount of money at the time."

"That was back before the day of the NASCAR plan, so there wasn't that much purse money," Humpy says. "We would set aside what we called 'deal money.' Earnhardt was a local guy. It was good for us to get him a chance. But, believe me, if Osterlund didn't want him in the car, he wouldn't have taken him for $5,000."

Osterlund decided he should meet this new driver. He went to a Sportsman race, watched Earnhardt banging around the track. Very nice. Humpy made the introductions at the end.

"And here was this ragtag guy," Osterlund says. "That's the only way I can describe him. This ragtag guy. I remember telling him once, 'You know that fashion the kids have with the holes in the knees of their jeans? You were there a long time before them.' I said, 'Jesus, criminy, where'd this guy come from?' He was divorced, on the verge of bankruptcy. And he wasn't even young. He was twenty-seven years old. That's the thing a lot of people forget. Dale Earnhardt didn't start out as a young rookie.

"He was something else. I have a painting of him now in my office from that time. The artist did a wonderful job. It's such a different picture of what you see in most of the pictures of him today. You see Dale as he was as a wild young man."

This was that Holiday Inn moment. The wild, young-but-not-really-young man had his chance.

He actually ran two races for Osterlund in '78. The first was in October in Charlotte, a Sportsman's race. Driving a car put together with spare parts in the Osterlund garage, he finished second to Bobby Allison. Then, in November, driving virtually the same car in the last Winston Cup race in Atlanta, he finished fourth. A possible plan to run two Osterlund cars in the next season ended when Marcis quit in the off-season. That left Earnhardt as Osterlund's one driver.

The fun began.

"We cleaned up a lot of situations for him, bailed him out of a lot of stuff," Osterlund says. "He was pretty much upside down when we started. He had an ex-wife on his ass for child support, bills everywhere. We funded a lot of stuff for him. We got him on a budget. Eventually we even put him in a house. That was my business, construction, so we set him up in the house on Lake Norman. He wasn't too excited about it, especially when he learned you had to make those house payments. He screamed and moaned, but he grew to love the place. Had a boat, the dock. The whole thing. He essentially became part of my family. That was how I felt about him."

Earnhardt was worried about running the whole circuit, because NASCAR now included a couple of road races. He had no experience with road races. ("You have to turn the wrong way," he said.) Osterlund brought him out to California to train in Bob Bondurant's driving school, learn the wrong-turn ins and wrong-turn outs of a road course like the one he would see in Riverside in the first race of the season.

Family. Osterlund brought Earnhardt to his house in California. Osterlund brought Earnhardt to his fifty-foot vacation houseboat in California. California! Houseboat! It all was a long way from Kannapolis.

"We drove down to the houseboat on the freeways," Osterlund says. "It was a long way, going through Sacramento, San Francisco, San Jose. Dale was driving. When he hit the traffic, he just pulled over to the side. He said, 'I can't drive in this.' He wouldn't drive. Then he gets to the houseboat, gets behind the wheel, and tries to do loops with it."

The situation was exactly what Earnhardt always had wanted. Better. He had a man with money—a friend, even, a man who considered him part of the family—and the man wanted to spend that money on racing. The worrying about money, about parts, about equipment, could stop. The man just wanted him to go fast. He was very good at that. He could go fast.

Starting with the first race at Riverside, rolling through the turns with two wheels on the grass half the time, making his own way, finishing a respectable 10th, he came onto the scene with an aggressiveness and fearlessness that hadn't been seen in a while. He brought the dirt track with him to the big time.

"He hit just about every wall on every track we went to," Osterlund says. "He darn near killed himself at Pocono. What you had to know was that Dale Earnhardt was expensive. A lot of people couldn't afford him, he wrecked so many cars. Bud Moore, after me, said he couldn't afford him. Richard Childress, after Bud, couldn't afford him the first time. It cost a lot of money to keep Dale Earnhardt on the racetrack."

Jim Delaney was an old mechanic who worked on the Osterlund cars during the week. He didn't go to the races. When the two-car hauler returned from Martinsville or Richmond or Talladega, Delaney would watch the carnage being unloaded. The cars would be twisted and bent puzzles that had to be solved. Sometimes both cars would be mangled. Delaney would take a puff on his corncob pipe and begin working.

"That's OK," he'd say. "Break 'em down and we'll put 'em back together. It's worth it. 'Cause we've got a good'un here."

"Speed didn't bother Dale," Wlodyka says. "There are a lot of drivers, successful drivers, they use up a lot of energy worrying about the speed. Dale always was in control. There were a lot of race car drivers who were scared to death of what he was doing."

"I think early in his career, he thought that the race car was a part of him," Benny Phillips, a friend and sportswriter from the *High Point Enterprise* (North Carolina), says. "He thought nothing could hurt him. Later, I think he changed his perspective. He'd had enough wrecks, enough experience. I don't think it slowed him down any, but I think he knew that you could get hurt in that car."

The young-man approach was exactly what Osterlund wanted. The payoff came in only the seventh race of the year, April Fool's Day, at Bristol in the Southeastern 500. Starting ninth, helped by a crash that took out polesitter Buddy Baker and veteran Cale Yarborough, Earn-hardt roared to his first Winston Cup win in the tidy half-mile track, beating Bobby Allison by three seconds. There was nothing fluky about the win. He'd led 160 laps, pulled away after the last pit stop with 23 laps remaining.

After taking an extra-slow victory lap, sucking in the moment at last, after all the years dreaming about it, he talked to reporters about how much this meant to him, and about how he thought about his father at the end. He said, "This is the big leagues." He was the fourth rookie in NASCAR history to win a race. It was his one win of the year.

"Every story you ever read about that season always talks about that win," Osterlund says. "But it's never mentioned how close he came in Texas. He should have won down there. He was leading with just a few laps to go, everybody just about out of gas or tires, final pit stop, and someone didn't tighten two lug nuts. The lug nuts flew off and the tires went flat and Dale damn near crashed the car, but he still finished the race."

And then there was Pocono.

This was another flat tire. Coming into turn two, known as the Tun-nel Turn, leading the race, the tire blew and he hit the wall. When the car finally stopped, he was stuffed into a helicopter and hurried to East Stroudsburg Hospital, where he was treated for two broken collarbones, a concussion, and severe bruises of the neck and chest. Doctors told him he was lucky he hadn't broken his neck.

"Where he hit, there was some signage along the wall," Osterlund says. "The side of his helmet was now the same color as the paint from the signage. That was how lucky he was to still be alive."

The injuries kept him out of the car for four weeks and he was replaced by successful veteran David Pearson, who won a race at Dar-lington. Earnhardt fretted, worrying that Osterlund would decide to keep Pearson in the ride, but the businessman was committed to his ragtag discovery. When Earnhardt had healed, he was back behind the wheel.

He put together top ten finishes in seven of the eight remaining races of the year, finishing seventh in the chase for the Winston Cup championship. He was named Rookie of the Year. He won purses totaling $264,086, a rookie record. The points finish was three slots lower than Marcis had finished a year earlier, but that did not bother Osterlund. He liked Earnhardt's style. He had found his man.

When the Junior Johnson operation started inquiring about the young driver's availability for the coming season, Osterlund quickly responded with the offer of a five-year contract. Earnhardt agreed. This was what he always wanted.

———————

"There were a bunch of us living in a trailer at the Car-O-Winds trailer park at the Frog Creek Camp Grounds," Doug Richert says, describing what came next in 1980. "Dale was living on the lake, but we were in the trailer. We'd hitch it up every week, the rest of us, and just go to where the next race was.

"It was like the circus. You go to the new town, stop, set up your stall, and try to win the balloon. We won the balloon."

Richert was a twenty-year-old California kid. He was another car junkie, West Coast version, not much for school, but in love with the workings of the internal combustion engine. He had been a friend of Osterlund's middle daughter, the one who loved the driver, and hooked up with her father at the beginning. When the father came East with Wlodyka, he took Richert with him.

"I really didn't know anything about NASCAR," Richert says. "I'd never seen a race. Except on television."

He was part of the pit crew. Osterlund had installed veteran mechanic Jake "Suitcase" Elder as the crew chief early in '79, but instructed Richert to pay attention to everything Elder did. There was a reason Elder was nicknamed Suitcase. He had a history of bailing out from assorted teams for assorted reasons. Unable to read or write, he nevertheless was a wizard with engines and cars. Osterlund told Richert to learn as much as possible from the master because someday the master will be leaving.

"I want you ready," the businessman said.

Coming off the promising '79 season, the team and Earnhardt now had some experience to add to bug-eyed ambition. There was an easy confidence. Riverside? The road course? The place Earnhardt had feared a year earlier, going to driving school just to learn how to run it? In the first race of the year, he took the pole and then finished second to Waltrip in the race. Daytona? He won his first Busch qualifying race, edging Waltrip, then finished fourth in the Daytona 500 after leading the race seven different times. Richmond? Fifth. Rockingham? Third.

In the fifth race of the year, the Atlanta 500, he climbed from 31st at the start to win by nine seconds over Rusty Wallace for his first win on a superspeedway. In the sixth race, at Bristol—hey, he'd won at this place a year ago—he won again by an impressive 8.7 seconds over Waltrip. This stuff was easy. He was leading the Winston Cup standings and cruising and . . .

Elder quit on May 26, the day after the Charlotte 600. Elder said he just couldn't get along with the sometimes abrasive Wlodyka. The kid, Richert, was now in charge.

"I had confidence in him," Osterlund says. "I thought he was ready."

"I never thought about being young," Richert says. "There was too much to do. I just wanted to keep everything going the way it had gone."

This, again, was new to the Winston Cup. A second-year driver leading the pack? Never happened. A twenty-year-old crew chief? From California? Ridiculous. It looked like some damn hippie kids had taken charge. They hung out, rode dirt bikes and water-skied for recreation, checked out the interesting parts of this new life they were living, then came out on Sunday and blew people's doors off.

"I thought we had the best driver in Winston Cup outside of Richard

Petty," Osterlund says. "The good ones, they seem to have that little thing in the solar plexus, that little switch in their heads that makes them go at the proper moment, to ask for one more thing, to say 'Goddamn, I gotta do it.' Dale had it, for sure. The difference with him was that he'd use it a lot earlier in the race than everybody else. He'd turn the switch halfway through while other guys were waiting for the end.

"He smoothed it off over the years, but I think guys back then were afraid of him. He ran over you. He didn't have that polish. When he came up on guys, they knew what was going to happen. They just let him through. We always finished pretty good, probably because of the other drivers' fears."

The points race came down to a battle between Earnhardt and Yarborough, the champion in three of the past four years while driving for Junior Johnson. Earnhardt was always the leader down the homestretch of the schedule, but Yarborough would close in or drop back with the finish of each week's race. This was a battle to the last checkered flag in Ontario.

"The race that put us in position to win came with four weeks left at Charlotte," Wlodyka says. "Dale and Cale were running very close at the front. It was one of those races with few caution flags, and fuel was going to be a problem. Everyone was going to have to pit. With about 29 laps to go, I saw that no one was in the pits and I called Dale in. I thought maybe we could get him in and out in a hurry that way, no one else around.

"That was what we did. By the time Junior saw what we were doing, it was too late. He brought Cale in the next time around, but there were four cars already in the pits. We won the race with that pit stop. Cale was second."

The lead at the final race at Ontario was down to 29 points after Yarborough won a week earlier in Atlanta, Earnhardt third. Position between the two racers was everything in this final race. This race also was almost decided in the pits. The other way.

"NASCAR probably won the championship for us, now that I look back at it," Wlodyka says. "If they hadn't black-flagged us, we never would have won."

First, Earnhardt lost a lap by coming into the pits too early during a yellow-flag caution. He regained the lap, but near the end of the race on a final gas-only stop, three lug nuts were mistakenly removed from the right rear tire. Earnhardt took off and NASCAR officials called him back.

"If they hadn't done that, hadn't spotted it, we never would have finished the race," Wlodyka says. "A wheel would have come off, an axle would have broken, something. He came back, we put on the lug nuts, and he went out and finished close enough to Yarborough to win the title."

Earnhardt finished fifth. Yarborough finished third. The final difference in the standings, after driving in 31 races all around the country, coast to coast, was 19 points. The ragtag dirt car driver from Kannapolis was the champion, a little over two years after being flat broke. His winnings for the season were $588,926.

"We were lucky," he said in his press conference. "I think we had help from a Higher Source." He did not specify whether he meant God or NASCAR.

The winning crew in yellow Goodyear shirts, arms and index fingers raised in a circle of No. 1's, looked like a high school baseball team in a postrace photo after winning the state title. The team from the Frog Creek Camp Grounds takes it all! Earnhardt, wearing a leather vest and bell-bottom jeans and cowboy boots, looked no younger.

He and his two brothers took off to Las Vegas for a night of celebration. It seemed like what you were supposed to do.

———

An article in *The New York Times* on August 4, 1980, probably described his life during these early days at high altitude as well as anything. A young woman sportswriter, Carrie Seidman, did the interviewing and writing. Earnhardt was twenty-nine, single, richer than he ever had imagined possible. Country charm drips between the lines. Is that a leer from the NASCAR champ in the background as he describes himself to the young woman from New York?

"He speaks with longing fondness of a party he threw before the Charlotte 600 in May that he hopes will become an annual tradition," Seidman reported. "There were almost 600 guests, 'all by invitation only, and all friends.' The group included other drivers and their wives, local pals and, without incident, his former wife, his current girlfriend and several other interested women. The tab ran to more than $1,000 and included the cost of sixty-some cases of beer, untold gallons of hard liquor and a rousing country-rock band. (Like his racing buddies, Earnhardt prefers his drinking, his women, and his cars fast and in quantity. . . .)

"There are frequent visits to Kannapolis to pick up his children for a trip to the lake, and the first time a sad expression crosses his usually carefree face during a long conversation is when he talks about wanting to bring them to live with him," Seidman continued. "He hopes to find a live-in housekeeper to fulfill that desire, but treasures his freedom too much to marry. 'Seems like every girl I go out with is either bitchin' or wantin' to get married,' he complains. He scowls when he thinks about finding 'the right one,' because that will mean he'll have to marry again. . . .

"Earnhardt has no intention of knocking himself out of the competition any time soon. There are too many more fish to be caught while knocking down a few cold ones on a glassy lake, under a basket of stars hanging on a humid North Carolina night, too many more deer to be stalked in the off-season with his little black mutt, Killer, and ways to be dreamed up to cook the venison. There are too many more hours to spend watching his children grow taller and smarter, and too many more women to entice his imagination. But, most of all, there are too many more races to be won. More than anything, his world is the world of speed."

This was the good ol' boy image that was appealing from the start. The language is bent in folksy directions, filtered through a nice molasses accent. There is a balance between driving fast and talking slow, between staying up late and getting up early, between hugging your kids and hugging the waitress. The drinking part probably is overstated—"I never saw him drink," Osterlund says. "If Dale Earnhardt was a drinker, it would have been a disaster"—but the rest rings true. This was the way he was.

"What do you think of when you hear the term 'redneck'?" Humpy Wheeler says. "If you're from the North, it probably is a bad term, perhaps implying bigotry or lack of intelligence, something like that. Which is a valid opinion. In the South, though, it's not so negative. It has different implications. There's a saying, 'He's a little red.' That's a good thing, to be 'a little red.' Dale was 'a little red.'

"I always think of him, for some reason, as the last Confederate soldier, sort of heroic, bound by honor. Johnny Reb. Dale Earnhardt was Johnny Reb. He was the last of a breed.

"When he went into Winston Cup . . . Winston Cup was much different from the way it is today. I looked at a picture of Jeff Gordon's winning team a few years ago, forty people, not one of them came from the South. When Dale came along, almost everybody was from the South. It was very much a closed society. When a black driver would come to race, I told him to think twice before he yelled about discrimination. There might be discrimination, but it also very well could be that what he thought was discrimination was simply the way NASCAR people treated *everybody* from the outside. This was a tight, closed group. And Dale? Dale had no problems. He had grown up right in the middle of it."

This was Dale before neckties. This was Dale before endorsements and business meetings. This was Dale before public relations handlers. This was Dale before commitments. He was as unvarnished and fresh, blinking in front of the camera, as the winner of Megabucks on a Saturday night. He just did what he did. Forget the consequences.

"Dale was very bright—his mind just needed to be exercised," Osterlund says. "He was also suave. He had that quality, no matter what he did, you had to like him. He could win that race at Bristol and everyone else in the race would be just cursing him out and he was like the little kid with his hand caught in the cookie jar. Who, me?"

This could go on forever. Couldn't it?

———————

"I've never explained this, except to my family," Osterlund says. "The next year, I was involved in a big building project on the West Coast. There was a bank out there that had been very good to me, had funded many of the things I had done. I wanted to stay on good relations with the bank.

"One of the officers came to me and said he thought I was stretching myself a little thin, traveling back and forth across the country the way I was, that I was going to kill myself. I got the message. I had to choose between the racing and the development business."

What to do? Already, there was a bidder for the racing operation. J. D. Stacy, a big-talking coal mine baron who smoked foot-long cigars and lusted for a championship, was in the process of buying up the NASCAR countryside. The Osterlund operation, defending champs, was an obvious target.

Osterlund thought and thought and took the offer. He was a West Coast guy and stayed on the West Coast. He didn't even fly to Derita to announce the news. He sent a message for Wlodyka to deliver.

"I couldn't go back there," Osterlund says. "I knew that if I ever was in a room with all those people I never could go through with it. Looking back, hindsight, that's probably what I should have done, gone back and been talked out of it, but it's too late now. I know Dale was upset. Everybody was upset. I think Dale understood, later in life, when he was in business, himself, but I know he was mad."

Everybody was mad. The family was gone. Stacy came onto the scene and installed his own man, Boobie Harrington, as the head of the operation, like it or leave it, fired six members of the crew, like it or leave it, took charge, and *wasn't even a racing guy.* Stacy would go on to buy up five different race teams, virtually race against himself in a lot of ways, looking for a title he never would win. It was a mess.

"Here's this guy, has no idea what he's doing," Richert says. "Just comes in and he owns you. You felt like a piece of cattle."

"I wound up eventually going back to California with Rod," Wlodyka says. "I became the food and beverage manager at his country club. Probably the worst decision I ever made."

The happy ride of youth was done. Earnhardt drove four races for Stacy and walked away.

There wouldn't be another championship for six years. The ragtag kid would be a thirty-five-year-old family man. It all would be different.

Roots . . . the young
Dale (left) with his
brothers Danny and
Randy, in front
of his father's No. 8
dirt-track race car.
The sport was part
of daily life.

Ralph Earnhardt,
local legend.

Dale, a racer at last, off to find
his fortune. He always knew what he
wanted, just wasn't sure how to get it.

NASCAR champion, 1980 (and the first driver to win the following year's title after capturing the Rookie of the Year Award).

New replaces old. Dale (3) battles Richard Petty (43) in Daytona qualifying in 1985. The two men would each win seven NASCAR titles in their careers.

Family man. Dale poses with Kelley (left), Dale Jr., and Teresa at Martinsville in 1987.

The outdoorsman. He hunted, he fished, he sat on the dock of his early home on Lake Norman and thought about hunting and fishing. His uncle, Dub Coleman, said Dale "had an amazing ability to remain still" while hunting.

On stage at the Waldorf-Astoria in New York with his seventh and final Winston Cup championship trophy. Rivalries and friendships were the fuel of his NASCAR life.

With Richard Petty.

With Darrell Waltrip.

With Richard Childress.

Neil Bonnett.

The track was his home. Dale waits for the start of the California 500 in 1997.

The most fearsome sight on the race-track: the black No. 3 Monte Carlo coming from behind.

Dale Jr., Dale, and Kerry at Michigan in 2000, the only time two brothers and their dad have competed in the same Winston Cup race.

The rise of Dale Jr. revitalized Dale's career.

At last, Daytona 1998. Dale wins
the one race that always had eluded him—
spraying champagne, accepting a kiss
from youngest daughter Taylor Nicole,
as wife Teresa smiles. This was the
biggest win of his career.

February 18, 2001. Dale walks to his car with Teresa. . . . He adjusts his goggles before putting on his helmet. . . . The DEI team finishes 1–2 with Michael Waltrip first and Dale Jr. second, but back on the Daytona track a puff of smoke signifies trouble. . . . Dale and Ken Schrader (36) hit the fourth-turn wall. . . . Rescue workers surround the No. 3 car. . . .

Teresa leaves the memorial service at Calvary Church in Charlotte.

Fans raise three fingers in the third-lap tribute that continued throughout the 2001 season.

The Intimidator. The Man in Black.

Students gather at Wofford College in Spartanburg, South Carolina, to form a No. 3 in honor of Dale.

5

Mark Martin is a pale man, slight, almost fragile at 5 feet 6, 135 pounds. This does not mean he is afraid to stare death in the eye. He is forty-two years old.

"Driving race cars is what I do for a living," he says in a quiet voice. "It's not for everybody. I know that. I wouldn't want to fight Mike Tyson. I wouldn't want to get trampled by those guys in the NBA. But I do do this. I do what I do."

This is Bristol, five weeks after Daytona, but the talk is still about mortality. There is no way to escape the talk about mortality. Not if you drive race cars.

"This is a reality check," Martin says. "This is probably the most profound reality check we've ever had to deal with. Dale is dead. How do you go on? You just do. You can't throw a switch on your life. You just go on."

Martin has made all the deals with himself, brought out all the rationalizations. You could get hit crossing the street going to the grocery store. The space shuttle could fall on your head. Things happen. You just keep going.

"Look, I want to be around for quite a while," he says. "I have a son who is nine years old. He needs me. I want to be here for at least the next ten years. I don't want anything to happen, but something can. That's part of our job. We all accept that."

Someone asks the pale, slight, almost fragile man how his life has changed since Dale Earnhardt died. The pale, slight, almost fragile man considers his answer.

"Every night, we pray for our family and the Earnhardt family," he finally says. "Before the accident, we just prayed for our family. I guess that's the difference. Now we pray for the Earnhardt family, too. . . ."

WINNING

The salesman always hopes for the good day, the magic twenty-four hours when his hair is perfect, when his business suit is rejection-proof, when doors are opened and he is greeted as if he were the answer to a long-mumbled prayer and the order book is filled. They don't happen often, sometimes never, these magic days, in a lifetime of indifference, but when and if they do they are memorable.

Richard Childress had a magic weekend. His life changed forever in the first weekend of August 1981 in a room at the Downtowner Motel in Anniston, Alabama.

"You look at what happened to him that weekend," Kirk Shelmerdine says. "He goes to Talladega for the race and he's struggling, going nowhere. He's driving his own car against the big teams. He has no money, no sponsors. Nothing. He goes to Talladega and, all in one weekend, he makes a deal with the Goodyear guy for tires, he signs a contract with GM that helps him get factory parts, and he signs up Dale Earnhardt as a driver and Dale brings a deal from Wrangler with him.

"That's some weekend, isn't it? He starts out as an independent car owner and driver, almost broke, and he becomes the owner—retired as a driver—of a big team himself."

This one weekend turned out to be the beginnings of a stock car empire. In the next two decades, two school dropouts from the farthest economic edge of American society would make more money, accomplish more things in their sport than anyone ever had thought possible. Two dirt-poor men would wind up with fifty-foot boats and personal jet planes and farms and beef cattle, with e-ticket rides through life, cutting the lines to the best events and most important people, flying off to Saskatoon to hunt grizzly bears on a whim. And winning six Winston Cup championships.

"They were two guys with the same background, with the same aspirations, but they had different approaches," Shelmerdine says. "Earnhardt was the cowboy, the dirt-under-the-fingernails guy, moving ahead with just muscle. Forcing his way. Childress was more of a planner. At a young age, he'd learned that muscle didn't work. Muscle? Anybody can do that. He'd bounced around, seen every way people worked at things. He became incredibly lucky, things just went right for him as he went along, but he hit some home runs along the way, too. One of his biggest was Dale Earnhardt."

Five years older than Earnhardt, Childress was working on the same slim margin of the dream that Earnhardt had worked before meeting Osterlund. He was carrying the bills from the finance companies in his pocket as he drove around the race tracks in cars that were not fast enough to catch the famous names he was chasing.

If anything, he had come to the sport with fewer assets than Earnhardt. Earnhardt at least had his father in the beginning, Ralph, a course to follow. Childress had only his imagination.

He was the oldest of five kids on the south side of Winston-Salem. His father died when he was five. Like Earnhardt, he had dropped out of school in tenth grade and worked a succession of menial jobs. One of the jobs, as a kid, was selling peanuts and popcorn at Bowman Gray Stadium in Winston-Salem, a dirt track where he had fallen in love with the same dirt legends that Earnhardt had watched. He, too, wanted to be the next Curtis Turner or Lee Petty or any one of the three Flock brothers.

Following the same zigzag path as Earnhardt, he had been around racing since he was seventeen, scuffling for rides everywhere, putting together his own cars, and paying for them sometimes with the family food money. He was thirty-six years old now, though, twelve years on the Winston Cup circuit, 284 starts and zero wins, six finishes in the top five, and had come to the realization that there had to be a better way to do things.

The better way, alas, was to stop driving.

"It was the hardest decision I ever had to make, probably," he told the *Atlanta Journal and Constitution* in 1993. "If driving becomes part of your life, when you get out of it and watch that car going around without you, it's like you've lost your best friend."

He was approached by Earnhardt on the fateful weekend at Talladega. Earnhardt wanted to get out of his new relationship with Stacy. Earnhardt's sponsor, Wrangler jeans, also wanted to get out. Moving to Childress's car would make the move so easy that Earnhardt could be racing again the very next weekend. Money and credibility could arrive in an instant. All Childress had to do was give up his first, abiding love.

He talked first with Junior Johnson, who told him what he already knew, that there were more drivers around NASCAR than there were owners around NASCAR. He then met on Saturday night at the Downtowner Motel with Earnhardt and representatives from Wrangler and Goodyear and hammered out the deal. Earnhardt ran his last race for Stacy on Sunday, out with a broken transmission after 83 laps. Done. He was with Childress the next week in Charlotte.

"The money that Wrangler was paying to sponsor my car for the final 10 races of 1981 was the most money I ever had seen," Childress said in Frank Verhorn's book, *The Intimidator*, in 1991. "They were going to pay me so much a race and Goodyear was going to help us with the tires. I went out and hired a bunch of new people, some of them from Stacy's shop, and bought all new engines and the other stuff I needed to build good race cars.

"When it was over, I was in debt $150,000. I was in worse shape than I was to start with. I was just devastated by the amount of money I had spent. I knew I had to do it, though, and we impressed a lot of people. We almost won a couple of races and Dale led a lot of laps.

"Wrangler came back and put $75,000 more into the team to help me out. I had to carry the other $75,000 over, had to finance it and hock about everything I had to make it work."

This was an entirely different game from the one Childress had played as a driver. He was inside the velvet ropes with the big boys now after looking from the other side for so many years. He could combine all of his ideas with all of the hard lessons he had learned. He was a player.

"Richard knew what he wanted from the beginning," Shelmerdine, eventually Childress's crew chief, says. "He was looking ten years down the line. He always had a plan. He was convinced that you had to build your own cars from the ground up. To do anything else was to be predictably mediocre. Getting Dale was the start—it put Childress on the map—but he knew how much work he had to do."

The amount of work forced Childress into a hard decision. Earnhardt ran 10 races to close out the '81 season, finishing six times in the top ten. This was good, probably better than expected for a team put together so fast, but at the end, Childress advised him to leave, to go to another, bigger team.

The two men were driving in Earnhardt's old Pontiac after qualifying for the Southern 500, the September race at Darlington. Earnhardt started talking about offers he'd had from other owners for the next season. The best offer seemed to be from veteran, big-time owner Bud Moore. Earnhardt asked Childress what he, Childress, would do. Childress told him to go.

It was a startling, honest appraisal between friends. The first year of a ten-year plan was no place for a NASCAR champion to be. He should go where his abilities would be better enhanced. OK? If the ten-year plan worked and if everything else worked out, maybe there could be a reunion, but for now the best move was somewhere else. OK? This no-nonsense judgment call by Childress set a standard for the future relationship. The two men always could and would tell each other the truth.

Earnhardt went off to drive for the high-profile Bud Moore Engineering team for two years, taking his Wrangler sponsor's money with him. It was a dissatisfying time, Moore running Fords, Earnhardt hating the Fords, the Fords breaking apart all the time. In 1982 he did not finish 18 of the 30 races he started. In 1983, he did not finish 13 of 30. He was back in the pack, 12th in the points race, in '82, eighth in '83. Frustrated, he won only three races in the two years he drove for Moore.

Childress hired driver Ricky Rudd. A sponsor appeared, Piedmont Airlines, and the ten-year plan began. Rudd finished ninth in the Cup standings for both years, winning two races in '83. These were Childress's first Cup wins.

"Ricky Rudd, it turned out, was a very good addition," Shelmerdine says. "For the two years, we were doing tons of development work. We were wide open into chassis construction. Ricky ran laps and laps of tests for us. He was good at that, probably better at that than at racing. You want a driver who is sensitive to the vehicle in testing, someone who notices the little changes. You almost want a driver who complains all the time. You want a dialogue. Dale was terrible at that. Ricky Rudd contributed a lot to the cars that Dale drove to championships."

After the '83 season, Childress re-signed Earnhardt. The ten-year plan seemed to be moving faster than anticipated. Rudd, dumped, hurt by the decision, wound up taking Earnhardt's place with the Bud Moore team. It all looked like a straight player deal in baseball. Except the two players were wearing the same denim uniforms. "We'd gotten more and more involved in NASCAR," former Wrangler jeans president Ed Bowman says. "We had three major areas to seek out Wrangler customers: the rodeo circuit, Willie Nelson and the country music thing, and NASCAR. Those were our people. We'd gone with Dale to Bud Moore. I had an overeager assistant at the time. When Dale left, we still had a deal with Bud Moore, but my assistant said, 'We've got to have Dale Earnhardt,' so he signed with Childress, too. Now we had two Wrangler cars in NASCAR."

Bowman remembers the deal with Childress costing "about $1.5 million a year," plus appearance money for Earnhardt, plus money to rent penthouse suites at every racetrack to entertain customers. It was an expensive proposition at the time. Bowman also remembers making loans to Childress.

"He'd need money to buy a part or something and we'd give it to him," Bowman says. "It was funny. One day I turned around and we weren't making loans to these guys anymore because they were rich. It seemed like it happened in a minute."

———————

The ten-year plan, the overall goal of the Childress operation, was to put a fearless driver into an unbreakable car. The adjectives in NASCAR are all about speed, but the trophies, in the end, are awarded for durability. Most Winston Cup races and certainly the overall points standings are testaments to endurance. The Childress cars were built for endurance.

"The American public operates from the myth that Dale Earnhardt made Richard Childress," Tribune syndicate automotive writer Ed Hinton says. "If anything, the absolute opposite is true. The cars Earnhardt drove in the eighties and into the nineties were the most bulletproof cars in the history of NASCAR. Had Childress not made the long-range commitment he did, none of the other stuff would have happened. Here was a guy, a rough driver who crashes a lot. He was put into cars that would stand up to the beating he gave them, that wouldn't break down."

The Childress garage eventually made every single part of every single car. The theory was that over-the-counter parts weren't good enough. None of them. The engine, the chassis, everything was built from the ground up. The parts were fabricated in the shop, put together in the shop. The cars were familiar puzzles put together with entirely new pieces.

"Nobody had done this, not the way we were doing it," Shelmerdine says. "We were totally unorganized. We had to guess at everything. Just shoot from the hip. There were twelve, maybe fifteen people playing iron-man football. We did a lot of stuff with the bodies, with the chassis. We had our own shocks made. We were always asking the factory guys, 'can you do this? Can you do that? Will it work for the long run?'"

Shelmerdine was Childress's crew chief, in charge of the iron-man football. He was another young guy, drawn to the engine noise from a Penn State dormitory room. What would you rather do, study for midterms or tackle Talladega? The lure was too much.

"When I was a kid, we lived in Dover, Delaware, for a while," he says. "Stock car racing wasn't that big in the Northeast, but I had a buddy who lived near the track in Dover. The Winston Cup would come every year, and we got into it. My family moved to Philadelphia, but I still loved the races. When I went to Penn State, I could see that college just wasn't for me. It was boring. My parents, I remember, came up to school. They said, 'Well, if you don't like this, what do you want to do?' I told them I wanted to go racing. I think they kind of gave me a pat on the back and said, 'Sure,' and waited for me to get over it, to come back. They're still waiting."

Nineteen years old, wanting to drive, Shelmerdine went to North Carolina. He wound up working as a gofer for James Hylton, a driver/owner in the back of the pack. That became Shelmerdine's education, doing bits of everything for Hylton, basically as the one employee on the payroll. He eventually moved to a spot as a mechanic with Childress, who wasn't in a much more successful position than Hylton at the time.

"He was just struggling when I got there in 1981," Shelmerdine says. "Everything he had was owned by the bank. It was a shoestring thing. Sponsorship was a necessity, but how did you get it? To attract a good sponsor you had to run in the front of the pack. To run in the front of the pack, you had to attract a good sponsor. How do you get out of that? When Richard did, that's when we were able to get rolling."

By the time the rolling started, Shelmerdine was the crew chief. A previous crew chief—shades of Jake Elder—had quit and Shelmerdine—shades of Doug Richert—was given the job "until someone else comes along." No one else ever came along.

Working on the automotive puzzles was as much fun as the young crew chief—twenty-two when Earnhardt and Wrangler came for good in '84—had ever had. There were possibilities to explore that don't exist today, holes in the rules that seemed like the Grand Canyon. Why isn't anyone else doing this? Let's try.

"There's a lot more rules today about what you can and can't do," Shelmerdine says. "It's all based on equalizing the field. I guess I can see what they're doing, but it changes the game, doesn't it? I mean, like in poker, you could make a rule that says 'no bluffing.' OK, but you don't have poker anymore. You've ruined the whole fucken game! Bluffing IS poker. That's what NASCAR has done with all its rules, taken away the game."

The Childress garage developed three different chassis for different

styles of tracks. Didn't that make sense? The tires were different sizes—
94 inches in circumference at the Talladega Airstrip, for instance, 82 at
tight little Martinsville—so shouldn't the chassis be different? The
geometry was entirely changed.

The tires were different in themselves. They would arrive from the
manufacturers with great, random variations in gripping ability. The
Childress garage would buy the tires in huge lots, then measure and
match, try to find fraternal twins in the random manufacture. What tire
worked better at short tracks, long tracks, intermediate? What tires
worked better in the summer, the spring? Logs were kept, tires matched,
dozens of tires simply rejected because they didn't match with anything.

Were other teams doing this? Who knew? There was no time to find
out. There was no inclination to give out secrets.

"What you want to do is win a race before it's even held, to make
the actual race redundant," Shelmderdine says. "That's what we wanted
to do. We wanted the car to be so good that the race was just a for-
mality."

For the first two full years in Earnhardt's return to the team, all of
this was being built, sorted out. He won two races in '84, four in '85,
finishing fourth and eighth in the points chase. By '86, the figuring out
was done. The Childress car was the best car on the circuit.

And it was being driven by the best driver.

———

"The best thing about Dale Earnhardt was that he loved winning car
races more than anything else in life," Shelmerdine says. "Nothing was
better in his book. If it was riding bicycles at the motel, racing slot cars,
fishing . . . anything, he wanted to win. The grin on his face when he
won said it all. The amount that he truly loved it, winning, that was his
strong suit.

"He was one ill son of a gun when he went on that track. You couldn't ask for anything more from a driver."

The priorities in Earnhardt's personal life had been reordered in the years since his Winston Cup championship season in 1980. In rapid succession, he had received custody of his two children, Kelley and Dale Jr., from his second marriage after their mother ran into financial problems with a devastating fire, and he had married Teresa Houston, the niece of sportsman driver Tommy Houston, on November 15, 1982, after proposing from his hospital bed after another crash at Pocono. The honky-tonk hero of *The New York Times* story still shook hands with a strongman's grip, still put friends and near strangers into bear hugs and headlocks, still roared through his days, but there was a governor on the engine now. Stability had entered his life for the first time since he quit school and started on his grand trip.

"Teresa won the race," Rod Osterlund says. "She was always around, but she was part of a group. Dale had a lot of women. He had women, I think, at every track during that 1980 season. Teresa did a smart thing. She became involved with his kids. Whenever they were around, she was taking care of them. This went on for a number of years. She got her man."

"They always liked each other," Tommy Houston says. "They were good for each other."

They became a team. Teresa, dark-haired and pretty, not only provided the domestic hand needed to run a family, but also brought solid business sense to the operation. She was a trusted, knowledgeable voice as the piles of money started coming through the doors, a role that would only grow larger as the piles became larger. Earnhardt, fearless and bold, riding those bumpers, pushing through those holes in the traffic, kept the piles coming. He found the spotlight and didn't let it go.

"The growth of Dale Earnhardt was incredible," Ed Bowman of Wrangler says. "When we first got involved with him, he was so shy around people he didn't know he couldn't hardly talk. If there was someone around who had more education . . . you could just see it with Dale, he was very uneasy. He felt inferior. As the years went by, though, he became better and better. Very good, in fact."

The 1986 season was the return to the top. The bulletproof man was driving those bulletproof cars. Fenders and bumpers were straight arms to move people out of the way. It had been noted that in three of his four victories in 1985 he had knocked contending drivers from his path, and when he knocked Darrell Waltrip into a spin, three laps remaining in the second race of 1986 at Richmond, both drivers losing a shot at the win, he established the way he was going to run all season long. NASCAR, not liking what it saw of that way, fined him $5,000 and put him on a year's probation, which later was rescinded.

"Nobody drove the way he did," Waltrip still says. "Nobody did the things he did. He took advantage of you. Put it this way, he would take a lot more than he would give. The idea was if you hit me once, I'll hit you twice. . . . He was very moody. Sometimes you would bump into him and it would be just racing, OK. Sometimes he would be coming after you."

The story for the entire '86 chase was Earnhardt and Waltrip, bumping fenders, trading words. Waltrip, the glib defending champ, was the press conference Muhammad Ali in the matchup. ("I'd put some psychological stuff in the papers, but it wouldn't do any good 'cause Dale and his boys can't read," he said.) Earnhardt was the no-nonsense Joe Frazier, wanting to fight for the championship on the track instead of the newspaper. ("I can read," he replied. "Just like in a kid's early reader. See Darrell run his mouth. See Darrell fall.")

It was all funny stuff, and Darrell did, indeed, fall in the next-to-last race of the year in Atlanta. Earnhardt won the race. Waltrip went out on lap 85 with a blown engine. Earnhardt had won five races on the season and was the Winston Cup champion. He was back. Back? He then rolled into the '87 season and just blew away the field.

"Those were the two great years," Shelmerdine says. "In '86–'87, we had the best stuff out there. No one could touch us. We came out in '87 and won six of the first eight races and we had the other two wired, just didn't win in the end."

The race for the '87 points championship had no drama at all after those first eight weeks, Earnhardt winning 11 times on the season, clinching the title at Rockingham with two races remaining. The drama was saved for the Winston, the midseason all-star show that Humpy Wheeler had invented for his track in Charlotte. That was the site of what came to be known as "The Pass in the Grass," perhaps Earnhardt's most famous driving move.

In the 10-lap Shootout final, after the two longer qualifying races had been dominated by Bill Elliott, Earnhardt took advantage of a first-lap bump between Elliott and Geoff Bodine to grab the lead. Elliott, convinced that Earnhardt had caused the bump, took off in pursuit. He banged into Earnhardt and Earnhardt banged back and that was the general theme of the race, Elliott and Earnhardt banging into each other. The memorable moment came when Elliott forced Earnhardt low, off the track and onto the strip of grass between the track and pit road. Earnhardt, hurtling along at straightaway speed, never flinched, keeping control and moving the car back onto the track to ride to the ultimate win. Both Elliott and Bodine were so mad they rammed Earnhardt's car after the finish.

NASCAR fined Earnhardt and Elliott, plus Bodine, for good measure. Elliott fumed and said, "If a man has to run over you, it's time to stop. I'm sick of it." Humpy Wheeler exulted.

"The greatest move in the history of auto racing," he said. "To be driving a car that fast on the grass? To keep control? That was unbelievable."

The greatest 1987 move of all, however, the move that affected Earnhardt's future more than any other, probably took place in the boardrooms of two American companies. The No. 3 car of Richard Childress—the number that still was remembered at that time mostly as the number on the side of Junior Johnson's car through a short but storied career—would have a different sponsor and a different color.

The Man in Black was being created. The No. 3 car would have entirely different perceptions.

"We had the defending champion," Ed Bowman of Wrangler laments. "We had another year to go on our contract. And our company, Blue Bell, was sold to VF, another company. VF came in, looked at NASCAR, and said, 'We don't want to do that.' Simple as that. We walked . . . from the defending champion."

The replacement was GM Goodwrench. This seems like a natural fit today—the parts division of a large motor company sponsoring a championship car that uses auto parts and has mechanics on national television—but in 1987 it was a shaky concept. Goodwrench never had been the main sponsor of a race car. Archie Long was taking a gamble.

"I wasn't sure I wanted to do this," the former head of the Goodwrench division of GM says. "I had a budget and I thought I probably could spend my money better elsewhere. I came to the races, though, met the people, and I soon found out I was dead wrong. This was really a form of advertising, a way to get the name out. We had some other people we were considering—Kenny Schrader was one of them—but we settled on Dale.

"In fact, I stuck my neck out. The president of GM didn't think we should do it. I said to him, 'Isn't the advertising budget my money?' He said, 'Yes it is.' I said, 'Can I do what I want with it?' He said, 'Yes.' So I said, 'Well, we'll just do it.'"

The decision created probably the most successful athlete/sponsor marriage in history. Has any one man or team ever been more closely tied to one product as Dale Earnhardt was to Goodwrench? If Earnhardt won, Goodwrench won. If Earnhardt wrecked, Goodwrench won. If

Earnhardt talked, walked, stopped for tires, Goodwrench won. Good-wrench won if Earnhardt did anything.

A key decision came from the styling section at GM. The blue and yellow color scheme of Wrangler jarred a few eyes. A suggestion was made to change the color to black. This was a big change. There never had been many Winston Cup cars painted black. Buddy Baker had driven one for a couple of years for an owner who liked the Oakland Raiders, but that was about it. Black was considered bland. The asphalt on the track was black. Wouldn't a black car sort of disappear into the asphalt? The stylists said it wouldn't. Black was now cool.

"The big movie those days was *Star Wars*," Archie Long says. "The kids all liked Darth Vader. That's what the stylists noticed. The car really became black because of Darth Vader."

And in the role of Darth . . . it all just seemed to fit.

————————

The next five years were a time of change for the Richard Childress Racing team. What do you do if you reach the goal in your ten-year plan after the first six years? The money started to pour in and the thrill of building, getting to the top, became the uneasy business of staying at the top. How do you plan for the future when you have to defend the present?

Childress built a new and modern racing complex in Welcome, North Carolina, outside Winston-Salem. He hired more and more people. The locker-room mentality of iron-man football was harder to maintain. The money, the success, changed the atmosphere.

"It's what's happened throughout NASCAR, nobody wants the trophies anymore, they want the money," Shelmerdine says. "To me, the money was always secondary. You get into racing to win races, to beat the other guy. What I always wanted was that cheap trophy with the plastic car on the top. That was racing. Winning the trophy.

When you're worth millions of dollars, though, that doesn't become as important."

For example, the Goodwrench people wanted to win the pole, to start first in races. Archie Long says, "We wanted to see our name at the start of the race, right up there. That's advertising, getting your name in front." The Childress cars never had been built to win poles. They had been built for the long haul.

"We never were good at qualifying," Shelmerdine says. "We didn't build the fastest cars. The car that we ran in qualifying was the same car we ran in the race. There were other teams that concentrated on qualifying, but when the race came, they were right back with us. Because the speed we did for that one lap was the speed we were going to do for all the laps."

The five years were a constant walk on the tightrope of high expectations. The pressures had changed.

In 1988, the arrival of the tire wars doomed the effort. Upstart Hoosier tires came along to challenge Goodyear. The technology of tires changed completely. ("All that stuff we'd been doing with tires before?" Shelmerdine says. "You just threw it in the wastebasket. It didn't matter anymore.") Earnhardt finished third in the points standings.

In 1989, winning five races, he finished second by only 12 points to Rusty Wallace. He took the final race of the season in Atlanta, a dramatic win, but Wallace finished 15th, just high enough to win the title.

In 1990, Earnhardt won again, his fourth championship, tracking down Mark Martin in a season-long chase, catching him in Phoenix in the next-to-last race, then holding him off in the season finale at Atlanta. In 1991, the fifth championship arrived. This was a strange year where contenders seemed to eliminate themselves. Earnhardt and the No. 3 car were left with Miss Winston again in the end.

"Both '90 and '91, we won mostly because nobody else seemed to want it," Shelmerdine says. "The cars from Roush Racing were the best cars out there every week, but we just outran 'em enough times to win."

In 1992, the whole thing fell apart. A new kid, Alan Kulwicki, roared to the championship. Earnhardt finished a distant 12th. He won only one race the entire year, the Charlotte 600. ("And he wouldn't have won that if it were 500 miles instead of 600," Shelmerdine says. "He won that all by himself. He just got pissed and outlasted everyone in the last 100 miles.") The future that had been envisioned in the ten-year plan had become the past. Other teams had caught up, following their own ten-year plans. The Childress effort seemed stale.

Shelmerdine quit.

"Sooner or later, everybody was going to catch us," he says. "We were robbing Peter to pay Paul, surviving. It was time for me to get out. We'd won everything we could win. Where do you go from there? We'd already beat all the big guys."

He decided to shoot for the trophy with the plastic car on the top from a different direction. He became a driver, stepping down to the ARCA series and back into the low-budget life. He is still there, thirty-nine years old, hoping someday to get a Winston Cup ride.

"I have a friend who tells me I'm the Howard Roark of stock car racing," he says. "Do you read Ayn Rand? I never cared about the money. I just wanted the trophies. That's why I'm here in ARCA, I guess, holes in my shoes and trying to get that tattoo of the word 'mechanic' off my forehead."

The Earnhardt operation needed a boost.

———————

"I wasn't looking to change jobs," Andy Petree says. "I had been working for Leo Jackson for ten years, crew chief for Harry Gant's car, and I was happy. A mutual friend contacted me and asked if I would meet with Richard. And I did."

The meeting was with Childress on a Sunday at the shop in Welcome. Petree was surprised to see that Earnhardt also was there. Petree liked the idea that Earnhardt was that involved. The three men sat in the closed shop and talked about racing, about philosophies and goals. Petree liked what he heard. He decided on his drive home that he would take the job. He wanted to win championships and thought this was the place where he could do that.

Another frustrated driver, he'd grown up in Hickory, North Carolina, and gone to school with Dale Jarrett. They'd become involved in racing together, and when it had become time to decide who works on the car and who drives the car, well, Jarrett had the driving genes and driving name from his famous father, Ned. Petree had the adjustable wrench in his hand. That was the deal.

He had a different crew-chief style from Shelmerdine. Shelmerdine was laid back, philosophical. Petree was straight-ahead forceful. At first, he wondered if that style was going to work. He wondered how long he would be able to stick with the operation.

"The first six months were tough," he says. "Everybody had been there so long, they were a tight-knit group. They were used to a certain style, a certain way of doing things. When I'd push, they pushed back."

The operation was twice as large as the fifteen-man garage Petree had run for Leo Jackson. There was more money involved, more pressure. There also was a different car-building philosophy. Petree had arrived to say that the old concentration on endurance, on durability, had become a liability. He was a promoter of performance.

"Durability had become almost an obsession with these guys," he says. "Endurance racing certainly is what we do, but there comes a time when you have to push the envelope. This game is a constant evolution. You're always weighing performance against durability. You think you have the right formula, but all of a sudden you're getting beat. You have to change."

Petree pushed for more lightweight components. Childress and Earnhardt pushed back, asking him to prove his ideas. Push and push. This was the new dynamic. Petree wasn't afraid to push. He found himself in a number of corners with Earnhardt. That was where Earnhardt liked to go.

"One day he was on the track, practicing, and there was something I wanted to talk to him about when he finished," Petree says. "He pulled the car into the pits, jumped out, and was gone. Ten seconds and he was gone. I went looking for him."

Earnhardt was inside his trailer. The door was shut. Petree opened the door and stepped inside. The trailer was filled with businesspeople. Earnhardt was talking about some deal.

"I'm busy," Earnhardt said.

"I know you are, you're talking to me," Petree said.

"What?"

"I don't know what you're talking to these people about," Petree said, "but I'm here to talk to you about the goose that laid the golden egg."

They talked. They battled. They worked together. The situation was solved by an old antihistamine: winning.

The 1993 season was a repeat of the good seasons with Shelmerdine. Earnhardt started fast, winning six of the first 18 races, building a 234-point lead, then hung on at the end for his sixth championship. He bumped and banged—especially in a classic come-from-behind dance in the Charlotte 600 when he sent struggling Greg Sacks across the track and into the wall to bring out a needed caution flag—and drove a Polish victory lap, backwards, at Pocono in memory of Alan Kulwicki and Davey Allison, who had lost their lives in recent crashes of a plane and helicopter. A 10th-place finish at Atlanta held off winner Rusty Wallace's late charge at the end of the season.

"I remember the excitement of that final day," Petree says. "Slim lead in points, end of the year, I never had been in that spot. Dale was terrific. Mentally tough. He had such a confidence in his ability."

In 1994, there was no final-day excitement. The No. 3 car simply ran away from everybody. Ernie Irvan, the one contender, dropped out of the chase with a near-fatal crash at Michigan. Earnhardt, winning only four races, but second seven times and third six times, clinched his seventh title at Rockingham with two races remaining in the season.

Seventh title! The achievement moved Earnhardt to the first line in the all-time driving list. He was tied now with Richard Petty, the King himself, for most Winston Cup crowns. Seventh title! He was forty-three years old and at the top of his game. A daughter, Taylor Nicole, had been born in 1988. His first son, Kerry, from his first marriage had joined the family at home with Kelley and Dale Jr. Seventh title! The kid from Kannapolis—Ralph's kid—was as middle-aged successful in his field as anyone in the entire damn country.

He was at the absolute top of his game.

"He was just an incredible driver," Petree says. "Physically tough, mentally tough, tough. He could be The Man every year. Do you know how hard that is? You won't see many athletes be The Man every year. One year, two years, but every year? Dale Earnhardt was The Man every time he went on the racetrack."

Petree had a unique look at a racetrack once from Earnhardt's perspective. Still wanting to drive, racing when he had a chance, Petree drove Earnhardt's Busch car in a race at Martinsville. The car was set up the same way it would have been set up for Earnhardt. The only change the mechanic wanted to make was with the seat. Earnhardt, with his many quirks, sitting at his familiar Sunday-drive angle, used an old Jeep seat, a "banjo seat." Petree wanted to put a normal racing seat in the car for the race. Earnhardt balked.

"Noooo," he said. "My seat stays in my car. Either drive it that way or don't drive it."

So Petree drove 300 laps, sitting on the banjo seat, the Jeep seat. He found that he almost was lying down in the car. He also found, OK, he kind of liked it.

Who could argue with Dale Earnhardt? Seven titles. Six in a nine-year span. Who could argue with this kind of success?

He was the best. Maybe the best who ever lived.

6

AT THE ALTAR

The Confederate flag flies from a pole on the back of Chuck Sandifer's truck in the parking lot at Talladega. This is pretty much your normal Confederate flag, red and blue and white, except in the middle of these stars and bars there is a circle that surrounds the No. 3. The words "FEAR" and "LESS" are on either side of the circle.

This is a Dale Earnhardt Confederate flag.

"I'm not making any statement," Chuck Sandifer says. "I just saw this at a flea market and I thought it was neat. I don't think Dale was a bigot, not at all. And I'm not a bigot. I just liked the flag."

A forty-three-year-old housepainter from Birmingham, Sandifer gave his heart to Earnhardt a long time ago "because he reminded me of the Lone Ranger." Sandifer's girlfriend, Carol McClinton, says Sandifer has Earnhardt sheets, Earnhardt pillowcases, an Earnhardt com-

forter on his bed at home. She says the bedroom, matter of fact, is pretty much an Earnhardt shrine.

"I've got everything in that room," Sandifer says. "Here, wait, let me show you something I brought with me. I bring it to all the races."

He is a small, muscular man with his shirt off to show tattoos of a heart and a lightning bolt on his chest. He goes to the truck and brings out a leather-bound photo album. The album contains bubble-gum cards of racers, mainly Earnhardt. Sandifer goes through the plastic pages slowly, explaining the significance of each card. He stops at his prize page.

"Dale and Neil Bonnett," he says. "See those two cards? Both autographed. I read in 1988 in the paper that they were doing a signing up in Hueytown at a store that Neil Bonnett owned. I got up there early. They both signed. Nice guys."

He holds the book as if it were a holy relic. He says no matter how much these cards were worth, he wouldn't sell them for all the money in the world. . . .

NEIL

Neil Bonnett wanted to put bolts into his sternum. That is what Clyde Bolton remembers. Clyde was a sportswriter at the *Birmingham News,* visiting Bonnett's house. Bonnett, driving at Dover, Delaware, on the Winston Cup circuit, had crashed and was recovering from his injuries. The biggest injury was the broken sternum, the breastbone. What kind of force does that take? To break your breastbone? He had hit the steering wheel with his chest. He virtually had split his sternum in half. He was in a lot of pain.

"What do you think?" Bonnett asked. "Could a doctor take a metal plate and sort of bolt it across there? Sort of screw it in? That way I could get back to racing quicker."

"Neil, I'm getting clammy just thinking about it," Bolton said. "Hearing you talk this way . . . no."

Bonnett looked at him.

"No," Clyde Bolton said.

Dale Earnhardt had a friend.

————————

There are not a lot of drivers who are good friends in Winston Cup. They might do the photo shoots and might be thrown together at various events and certainly might have some shared workplace issues, but mostly the men who drive the cars take separate paths when the race day ends. There is too much competition involved, everyone out for himself every week, too many incidents that can happen, too many grudges to carry.

There also is the mortality factor. Do you want to get close to someone who might not be around in the near future? The death of an anonymous neighbor always is much easier to take than the death of someone whose lawn mower you borrow every weekend. Give your heart away and there is a very good chance in this business that it can be broken.

Earnhardt and Bonnett didn't worry about all that.

Earnhardt and Bonnett didn't worry about much of anything.

"Neil comes around one day and he's driving a new Town Car," Butch Nelson, a friend and business partner of Bonnett, says. "No, it's not a Town Car. It's a new Lincoln Continental Mark VIII. Beautiful car. No miles on it. New. Sitting in the front seat is a deer head. There's blood coming out of the deer head all over the upholstery. Blood really is everywhere. Did you ever try to get blood out of upholstery? You just can't do it."

"What's the deal?" Nelson asked.

"Isn't that just the biggest deer head you ever saw?" Bonnett replied, proud as could be.

Earnhardt and Bonnett. Bonnett and Earnhardt. They were cut out of the same bolt of unconventional cloth. Totally wacky, the two of them. They found each other on the old Sportsman's circuit and recognized their similiarites. *I'd do that. Yeah, well, I'd do that, too.* They were bonded, locked together for almost two decades. They started poor and ended rich and always were friends and always had fun.

They hunted, they fished. They just didn't care. They were immortal. When the money arrived, Dale winning championships and Neil driving in the big show and winning races, two grown-up twelve-year-old kids were ready with ideas on how to spend it. The internal combustion engine had been invented and built especially for them. They bought, borrowed, schmoozed their way into all manner of transportation. Boats. Trucks. Cars. Recreational vehicles. They took these motorized tools and made them into grand and happy toys.

They played rough with the toys.

"Neil shows up at Earnhardt's house, two o'clock in the morning, to go hunting," Mike Bolton, the outdoors editor of the *Birmingham News,* Clyde's son, says. "Neil has a brand-new Honda ATV with him. Beautiful. He's very proud of it.

"Earnhardt says, 'I gotta have one.' Neil, who owns a Honda dealership, says, 'Yeah, we can order you one.' Earnhardt says, 'No, you don't understand. I gotta have one now.'" They go to the nearest Honda dealership. They call the emergency number on the front door, wake up the manager, and he comes down in the middle of the night and sells Earnhardt an ATV like Neil's.

"Now they go hunting. The sun is starting to come up. Neil's driving the ATV down a path in the woods. He's real careful, because he's proud

of his new toy. Earnhardt's next to him. Fed up. Earnhardt just takes
a sharp right. He hits Neil, knocks him off the path, down a bank.
The ATV just rolls over and over. Neil goes flying. He's all cut up. The
ATV is dented and dirty. Earnhardt says, 'Well, maybe now we can do
some hunting. You won't have to be worried about getting scratches on
that ATV.'"

For as long as they knew each other, Bonnett almost seemed to be
the face in Earnhardt's mirror. He thought like Earnhardt. He drove like
Earnhardt. He laughed like Earnhardt. The two men had the same kind
of mustache, same southern drawl. Bonnett had more personality, finding it easier to talk to strangers. Earnhardt had more success, driving the
Childress cars to one championship after another.

Away from the track, away from the fans with autograph books,
away from the men in suits with contracts and deals, away from families, the two drivers could be anonymous and young. They reveled
in their freedom, brothers of the woods. It didn't matter if they talked,
didn't talk, if other people were with them or not. Everything was natural and easy. They were classic buddies, Butch and Sundance characters, laughing at life.

Earnhardt would buy a bass boat that would do 90 miles per hour.
Bonnett would by a bass boat that would do 110. ("You drive the boat
at 110 miles an hour, it really takes the fight out of a fish," he said.)
They would each buy bigger guns, better guns. They would spend
$25,000, $30,000 setting up an area to hunt, building elaborate blinds
and tree stands, staying in the woods for four and five days at a time.

Bonnett was Earnhardt. Earnhardt was Bonnett. Interchangeable.

Bonnett story: He was driving the 110-mph bass boat on a river
in Alabama one afternoon. He was driving somewhere around the
maximum, 110-mph speed. He decided to pull into a small marina for
something to eat, finishing the move with a fine fantail spray. A fish-
and-game policeman, a ranger, was waiting for him. The ranger wanted
to give Bonnett a ticket for excessive speed on the river.

"Do you know who I am?" Bonnett asked as the ranger began to write.

"No, I don't," the ranger replied. "And I don't care."

"No, really, do you know who I am?"

"No. And look, I don't care if you're the King of Siam. You're getting a ticket."

"You don't understand," Bonnett finally said. "You really don't know who I am?"

"No!" the policeman grunted.

"Fine," Neil Bonnett said as he gunned the 110-mph bass boat and escaped down the river. "That's all I wanted to know."

Bonnett story: He had a promotional deal to drive Chevy Suburbans. He would keep the Suburban for 5,000 miles and bring it back to the dealer in exchange for a new one. The idea was that NASCAR driver Neil Bonnett drives this vehicle and you can, too. You, in fact, if you make the deal right now, can drive the very vehicle that Neil Bonnett drove! The idea, alas, worked well only in theory.

"Neil would do awful things to those Suburbans," Butch Nelson says. "He'd go hunting. He'd drag all kinds of dead animals around in the back. The blood would get into the upholstery. There'd be scratches and dents on the sides of the thing. The Chevy dealer, I can still see this now, once had five Suburbans lined up in a row on the top of a hill. He couldn't sell a one of them. They each had only 5,000 miles, but Neil had beat 'em up so bad it was like they had 60,000. And the blood . . . you just can't get blood out of upholstery."

Bonnett story: Earnhardt showed up one day at Bonnett's dealership. Another trip for hunting. Another ATV story. Bonnett had ordered the newest ATV, black, four-wheel-drive, perfect, and charged it to Earnhardt. He presented it to him in the parking lot. Here, it's yours. You bought it. Earnhardt said that was fine with him. He would take it with them.

This was January, maybe fifteen degrees, maybe twenty, cold in Hueytown, Alabama. Earnhardt had driven down from Mooresville with a Suburban, pulling a trailer that held a Toyota pickup truck. The pickup was to be used in the hunt. Earnhardt's plan now was to put the ATV into the bed of the truck, making a convenient, carry-all package. He pulled out a couple of skids so he could drive the ATV onto the truck.

A sheet of ice, alas, had been added to the skids during the trip down from North Carolina. When he tried to drive the ATV onto the truck, he couldn't get more than halfway up the skids. He kept sliding. Bonnett had a suggestion.

"What you have to do," he said, "is get back a ways and maybe get the ATV going about 40 miles per hour. You get up the skids, then jam on the brakes. The ATV is in the truck. If you can do it."

Earnhardt said this was fine. Of course he could do it. He backed the ATV a reasonable distance away from the skids. He revved the engine. He took off, doing the 40 mph. What he didn't know—and Bonnett had noticed, even before he suggested this plan—was that two inches of ice also had formed in the bed of the truck.

Earnhardt hit the brakes and couldn't stop. He went flying over the handlebars. He hit the cab of the truck, blam, went into the air again, and landed, blam, on the hood of the Suburban.

"I saw it all," Butch Nelson says. "A lot of people from the shop saw it. He had to be hurt. There's no way he could have hit the way he did and not be hurt."

Earnhardt stood up and laughed. Never gave any indication of pain. Boys will be boys. This was fun. Bonnett was Earnhardt. Earnhardt was Bonnett.

Four years older than Earnhardt, Bonnett had started out as a pipefitter in Birmingham, working on tall buildings, walking the steel beams. He always said he turned to racing because it was a job that had less danger than pipe fitting. He also said he noticed that there was a line of people who wanted to take his job as a pipe fitter. No one, he said, wanted to take his job behind a steering wheel.

He started driving with his brother on weekends, ran out of money, then hooked up with Nelson, who owned a race car, then hooked up with the racing Allison family of Hueytown to become what was known as "the Alabama Gang," a group of drivers who did great things on the Winston Cup scene. He had the same fearless qualities as Earnhardt, the same sense of being invulnerable.

"Neil never cared a lot about money," Butch Nelson says. "He just wanted to have a good time."

Nelson had grown up in Hueytown with race car dreams, himself, driving go-karts, taking black-and-white pictures of the big-time racers of the fifties with his little Brownie camera. When he was old enough, he started thinking about driving in races. A big feature at the time was figure eight racing, an enterprise that was exciting because, well, there always was a pretty good chance that something interesting could happen at that intersection in the middle of the figure eight.

Nelson was almost finished building his car, when the thought hit him that, Jesus, a man could get killed or seriously hurt driving in the figure eights. Especially in that intersection. He found a local old boy who never had been bothered by that thought and they won a race on the very first night and then a race on the second, third, and fourth nights. Nelson's total winnings for the four races was over $5,000.

"Those days," he says, "if you had $5,000 you were richer than dirt. I went about building a car for regular races."

Picking up Bonnett as a driver was a big move. Bonnett was broke, quitting the sport, and Nelson said that was the wrong decision. Bonnett should quit his real job, pipe fitting, instead, and come to drive for Nelson. Bonnett said if he did that, his wife might kill him. Nelson told him, well, everybody knows that auto racing is a dangerous sport.

"We went everywhere, we beat everyone," Nelson says. "It's the most fun I ever had in my life."

There was a race. . . . OK, Bonnett was leading the race by two laps. This was the 186th lap out of 200. L. D. Ottinger, a big name on the circuit, had whacked Bonnett earlier, but Bonnett had survived and was leading the race. Was leading by two laps. Didn't need tires. Didn't need gas. Was going to win the race.

And came into the pits.

"What are you doing?" Nelson asked.

"I want to get behind Ottinger, lap him," Bonnett said. "I want to put him into the wall for what he did."

"But you're winning the race."

"There's a lot of chances to win races. You won't get a chance this good to get L. D. Ottinger for a long time."

"He comes up behind Ottinger, but Ottinger is too smart for him," Nelson says. "Ottinger knows what's coming. He jams on his brakes. Neil flies past him. Mad. He has to win the race anyway."

There was another race . . . Huntsville. A little quarter-mile track. All the big names were there. The Allisons. Ottinger. Darrell Waltrip. Harry Gant. Earnhardt. There was a rule at the time for quarter-mile tracks that crews had to use a four-way lug wrench. This caused more pit stops and much longer pit stops. Bonnett figured out a strategy. He wondered if you used really hard Hoosier tires, as opposed to the normal soft tires, you could run the entire race on one set of tires. You would have to run really slow, slower than everyone else, but if you never had to change tires . . .

"We couldn't even qualify the car with the tires, it was so slow, had to take a provisional just to get into the race," Nelson says. "Everybody just ran away from us, and by the 50th lap, we were a lap down. Then there was a caution, though, and everybody came into the pits. We stayed out, and by the time everybody came out, we'd gained three laps and now were ahead by two laps."

With 30 laps to go, to make the story short, same strategy through all the pit stops, the slowest car in the field was ahead by 16 laps.

Everybody was going crazy. Tony Eury Sr., the crew chief for Earnhardt, handed Butch Nelson a headset and said, "Dale wants to talk to you."

"Butch, when are you all going to stop for tires?" Earnhardt screamed.

"We're not," Nelson replied.

"I thought so," Earnhardt grumbled, adding some bad words.

Would have been a great strategy. Would have won the race. Except Bonnett hit the wall in the last few laps. Finished second. Oh, well. Figuring out the strategy was almost as much fun as winning the race.

"Neil had a great mind for stuff like that," Nelson says. "He was always looking at things a little different. He had great ideas."

Bonnett left Nelson to go to the big time with the Allisons and then Harry Hyde and an assortment of teams on the Winston Cup tour. He had good success as the seasons passed, 18 wins, 18 poles, a factor in most races, but like Earnhardt, he had a tendency to be in crashes. Unlike Earnhardt, he did not walk away from his crashes.

"Neil always claimed there was an art to crashing," Nelson says. "Something about getting the back end to hit first . . . but I don't know about that."

A crash in Charlotte in 1987 put Bonnett's career in jeopardy. Doctors told him he would be out for a year with a shattered leg. They put a plate in his hip. He was back in twelve weeks, then won the first three races of 1988. The crash in '89 kept him on the sidelines again with the broken sternum. A crash at Darlington in the spring of 1990 almost finished him.

Midway through the TransSouth 500, he was involved in a fourteen-car pileup. It did not look like a bad crash, mostly one of those jumbles of steel, but while everyone else walked away, Bonnett suffered serious head injuries. He suffered amnesia. He remembered everything that had happened since the race, but nothing that had happened prior to the start. He didn't recognize his wife, his children, his parents. He did not know what he did for a living.

Doctors told him that his memory probably would return but that he would never race again. The party was done.

———————

The first memory that came back involved Dale Earnhardt. They were hunting somewhere and they each had spotted a nine-point buck. They each were waiting in different parts of the woods. The buck finally came near Bonnett's field of fire and Bonnett shot him. The joy of that moment was the first thing that came back. Not family. Not racing. Not wedding bells or the birth of children or even a Winston Cup trophy. No. Running to tell Earnhardt about the buck. That was the memory. Running to collect the points in the constant overall score of life that the two men kept.

"I shot that deer when I was hunting with Dale," Bonnett said to his wife, Susan, reporting the sudden thought.

Slowly, the pieces of his life came back to him. A veil was removed. Hey, he was Neil Bonnett. He was a race car driver and famous. At the same time, he also began to forge a new life.

He already had his Honda dealership and a fish farm, and now he also became a television broadcaster. A good one. He was a color commentator for Winston Cup races and soon had his own show, *Winning,* on The Nashville Network. He had a character, Pepe deBonnett, on the show. It was a laugh.

The problem any athlete finds with retirement, though, is that it is a far different life as the former heavyweight champion of the world from being the present heavyweight champion of the world. The look in people's eyes is far different when they meet you. There is a certain irrelevancy to all you have done. You are yesterday's news. If you once were a race car driver and now are a broadcaster, sorry, you are a broadcaster. You live on the safe side of the fence now.

Bonnett, despite his success in his new life, felt all this. It bothered him.

The one driver who treated him the same was his friend Earnhardt. They still hunted, fished, talked all the time. Bonnett finally felt good, great, as well as he ever had felt. The doctors told him the amnesia was totally gone. Bonnett wanted to get back into a race car. Earnhardt had an opportunity.

The Childress team was going to switch from the successful Lumina to the new Chevy race car, the Monte Carlo, in 1994. This was 1993. The new car needed a lot of testing. Dale was too busy and, remember, wasn't the world's greatest test pilot. ("We need more power in the engine" was his big report after most tests, most trial runs with a new setup. Period.) Bonnett could do that job.

He began driving the new car at Talladega and wherever the tests were held, pushing it to its limits, taking it deep into the turns, rekindling that old rush of danger and speed. He loved it. This was the flat-out, balls-to-the-wall pace he'd always had to his life. He wanted more. He wanted to race again.

"What do you think?" he asked, closing the door to Butch Nelson's manager's office at Neil Bonnett Honda in Hueytown.

"I think, if you're silly enough to be testing cars, you might as well be racing them," Butch replied. "Testing cars is probably more dangerous than racing them. You're taking the car out at a speed you'd never be able to run in a race. That's one thing. The other, if you crash in a race, you usually take somebody with you. That cushions the blow, the other car. If you crash in a test, it's just you and the wall. Yeah, if you're going to test, you might as well race."

Most drivers cautioned Bonnett against a return. His wife didn't want him to do it. He was forty-six years old. Why even think about racing? Why bother? Neil Bonnett had made his mark already. Just live with that. Earnhardt, the friend, had the opposite voice. He was on the same side as Butch Nelson. Go for it. Earnhardt was Bonnett. Bonnett was Earnhardt. What would Earnhardt do if he were in Bonnett's situation? No debate.

Childress entered a backup car in the July race at Talladega with Bonnett as the driver. This was the chance.

The race was on July 25. On July 12, Bonnett was at Talladega working with David, his son. David also had become a driver. Neil was helping him work on the car and test it. While they worked, they heard the sound of a helicopter. Neil looked up and recognized the vehicle.

"That's Davey Allison's new helicopter," he said.

Davey was now the young hope of the Alabama Gang, which had been troubled in recent years by a near-biblical run of tragedy. Bobby, the Hall of Fame patriarch, had been involved in a crash and suffered a brain injury. Donnie, his brother, had been involved in another big crash and retired. Clifford, Bobby's son and Davey's brother, had been killed in a crash. Thirty-two years old, Davey was already a Daytona 500 winner, a top ten driver.

The helicopter was a Hughes 369 HS. Davey had soloed for only nine hours in it. He was taking a ride with Red Farmer, another driver from the Alabama Gang, and they decided, on a whim, to fly to Talladega to watch David Bonnett's practice runs. As they attempted to land, the helicopter suddenly shot up twenty-five feet, went into a violent counterclockwise motion, turned, and crashed. The Bonnetts heard the sound.

"What's that?" David asked.

"That's Davey Allison," Neil replied. "He just crashed."

Bonnett ran to the wreckage, turned off the helicopter's motor, and pulled both men from the cockpit. Farmer would survive, but Davey Allison, after four days in a coma, would die. Thirteen days after all of this started, Bonnett would return to racing at Talladega. He also would crash.

It was an awful-looking affair on lap 131. The car became airborne and was stopped from going into the stands only by the wire restraining fence. The race had to be stopped for an hour to fix the fence, but Bonnett not only walked away but finished the afternoon back in the broadcast booth. He felt great.

"The wreck wasn't as bad as it looked," he later said. "I came out of it with a positive attitude. It was at Talladega where I knew I had to keep racing. When I went out to qualify . . . and started down the straight-away, I started to cry. That's how much it meant to me.

"That's when I started planning to get a ride for the Daytona 500."

———————————

Five races. That was all. The Neil Bonnett Farewell Tour. He would hit the big spots in 1994—Daytona and Talladega and certainly Indianapolis, this new Brickyard 400—and wave to the masses and walk into the sunset. He would go back on the high wire just to show that he could do it. These last few times.

Daytona, of course, was the first race. The Daytona 500. Speed Week. This had always been an important stop on the perpetual playground, Bonnett and Earnhardt, Earnhardt and Bonnett. This was the home of NASCAR history. This was the home of fun.

"There's a lake in the middle of the Daytona International Speedway, Lake Lloyd," Mike Bolton, the outdoors editor, says. "It's only open to drivers and crews for fishing during Speed Week. There's a tournament. Earnhardt was out there one year, fishing, and found a huge bass caught up on a bed. He tried a variety of plugs to try to make the fish bite, but couldn't do it. He had this secret fish that certainly could win the tournament, but he couldn't get it out of the water. Against his better judgment, he discussed the problem with Bonnett."

"Let me see the fish," Bonnett said.

"This is my fish," Earnhardt said. "I don't want you doing anything with it."

"I won't do anything with it," Bonnett said. "Just show me the fish."

The two men looked into the two, three feet of water, and the fish was still there, caught on the bed. Bonnett tried to think, of course, what he could do with this situation to drive Earnhardt crazy. Earnhardt had to go to practice for the Grand National race, but Bonnett said he would figure out a solution. He was still sitting at the side of the lake when he saw Earnhardt involved in a large crash on the track. Pieces of the car flew everywhere. Bonnett had an idea.

He walked to the track. The safety crews were sweeping up the debris. He went and grabbed the battered hood of Earnhardt's battered car. He took the hood back to the lake, nudged the fish free, and put the hood in the water exactly where the fish had been.

"I couldn't do anything," Bonnett said when Earnhardt returned, straight from the track hospital. "I was sitting here, thinking about your problem, when all these pieces of your car came flying through the air. Scared the fish right off the bed."

Bonnett and Earnhardt. Fun. History.

On the first day of practice for the first 1994 race of his farewell tour, in the fourth turn of Daytona, Neil Bonnett crashed and died. Simple as that.

There would be many similarities noted with another crash that would happen exactly seven years and seven days later, maybe 200 yards down the track wall, but this was a moment that stood alone. Even when another driver, rookie Rodney Orr, crashed and died three days later, Neil Bonnett's death was different. This was a sign that anyone was vulnerable.

"Neil was the first driver who had won more than one Winston Cup race to die in more than thirty years," Butch Nelson says. "You had to go back to Fireball Roberts to find the last one. There were a lot of drivers to die—but Davey died in the helicopter and Alan Kulwicki died in a plane crash and everyone else hadn't won more than one race. Tiny Lund died, but he'd only won one."

NASCAR initially attributed the crash to "driver error," but Earnhardt and Bonnett's family fought that finding and it was later rescinded. The cause was a mystery. There was some talk that the new Hoosier tire was the culprit. There was other talk about the tension in the springs. There was the usual wonder if some small part had broken. The car was destroyed. Any answers went with it.

The members of the media caravan were shaken. Like the drivers, they have a tendency to stay at a business distance from the people behind the wheel simply because of circumstances like this. Bonnett was different. He had become one of them. He ate with them, hung around with them, bitched with them. This death was more "real," if that was the right word, than any of the other ones.

"I just wrote a story that Neil Bonnett is dead," a writer said incredulously in a house a bunch of NASCAR journalists shared at Daytona. "Can you believe it, boys? Neil Bonnett is dead."

Earnhardt, true to whatever code he had developed, went onto the Daytona track an hour after his friend died and practiced. He said he felt "numb." At the end of the week, true to the code, he raced in the Daytona 500. He qualified second and finished seventh.

Bonnett and Earnhardt had made a pact that they would not attend each other's funerals. The code. Earnhardt stayed with Bonnett's wife, Susan, the night of the accident, but did not go to the funeral in Hueytown as yet another member of the Alabama Gang was laid to rest. Grief was an emotion to be dealt with internally. The code.

Three weeks before the crash, Bonnett and Earnhardt had gone hunting with Mike Bolton. In 1986, Bonnett had called Bolton, a stranger, after Bolton wrote a story about an Alabama man who caught a record bass. Bonnett wondered if Bolton could take him fishing where the bass had been caught. Bolton agreed, thinking this might be a neat story, a day fishing with a NASCAR hero, and when Bonnett arrived, Earnhardt was with him. The day went well. They all had gone hunting and fishing together now a bunch of times.

On this latest trip, Bolton decided to take a picture of the two famous drivers. He is a short and portly man, and he lay down on the ground to take the picture from a different angle.

"Mike," Earnhardt said, "you're the only guy I know who's taller sideways than he is standing up."

When the NASCAR circus came to Talladega in the spring after the crash, Bolton went to see Earnhardt. They talked for a while, reminisced. Bolton had brought a copy of the picture. He thought Earnhardt would like it.

"I handed him that picture and he looked at it and then looked at me with the coldest look I've ever seen in my life," Bolton says. "He just stared for maybe forty-five seconds. Then he turned around and walked away. He left the picture. I wondered what I had done."

The innocence was gone. Earnhardt would move along and win the Winston Cup championship for the year, the seventh crown, but life was different. This was the biggest shock since the death of his father.

7

AT THE ALTAR

People began to write on the sides of the Dale Earnhardt souvenir tractor-trailer, a big black and silver and red eighteen-wheeler, the night after the accident. There was no stopping them. This wasn't graffiti, it was hieroglyphic need. People had things they had to say.

"Now you're racing for the Lord. Hope he don't put you in a Ford." Gina.

"There are no restrictor plates in Heaven. Dale will always have the pole. We will miss you." The Linehan Family.

"Have you accepted Jesus as your Savior? Dale did." Cool, N.C.

The other three Dale Earnhardt souvenir trucks had taken off shortly after the race, making the long trip from Daytona back to Charlotte. That is NASCAR life. Everyone leaves as soon as the race ends, a caravan of trucks that heads straight out the gate, mingling in the traf-

fic with the race fans. Terry and John Tull had decided even before the race to skip that, waiting to drive their truck back home in the morning. They found the writing when they arrived back at the track.

"It began then and hasn't stopped," Terry Tull says. "Our boss decided just to let people write whatever they wanted."

The NASCAR season is only a third of the way finished as she talks, but already every available spot is filled with Magic Marker words. The surfaces of the other three trailers also are filled. There is no more room, but people still find room.

"I miss you." Love, Alison.

"Damn it, Dale. Damn it." Zillot.

"He should not have been taken in the blink of an eye. Instead, allowed to fade off into the sunset with other heroes who would not die." Russ Weeks.

"Bobby Labonte signed the truck in the back," Terry Tull says. "He was like everyone else. Came here at Darlington and signed."

"Talladega will never be the same. #18."

BUSINESS

Hank Jones remembers he had a T-shirt for sale, maybe back in 1988, that called Dale Earnhardt "The Dominator." He remembers the T-shirt wasn't selling well, "just wasn't dominatin'." He remembers he needed a new name for his man. What could it be? He thought long and hard.

"I came up with the name 'The Intimidator,'" Hank Jones says. "Dale wasn't real hot on it. I said, 'Well, that's what you are, you know?

Even when you don't win, the way you drive, you're just intimidating everyone else out there on the track.' Dale still wasn't real hot on it, but he gave me the go-ahead and we printed up some real nice shirts and they just took off. The name caught on with fans and it caught on with the other drivers. They started calling him 'The Intimidator.' Everybody did."

The Intimidator.

There probably are more glittering examples of the proper name attatched to the proper product in the marketing courses in the business schools of America—somebody had to call that sugary brown liquid "Coca-Cola" and someone had to say, "I think we'll call our cameras and film 'Kodak'"—but in a down-home, sports merchandising approach, the nickname Hank Jones found for Earnhardt was as good as any. Man plus image equaled bucks. More bucks than anyone ever had thought possible for driving a race car around and around.

From a basic beginning philosphy of economics that wasn't much different from his dad's philosophy—win races, win purses, maybe pick up a little money on the side—Earnhardt became a broad-based millionaire. A guy with an eighth-grade education met a guy with a sixth-grade education and, together, they pretty much were business pioneers. They opened up financial doors that never had been opened in NASCAR. They followed the paths of the old snake-oil salesmen of the West, traveling in modern heavy equipment, opening the side doors and selling modern doodads and trinkets and baseball caps to keep out the sun. They created a need and they filled that need, thousands of times over.

The timing was right and the people were right and the product was right.

"It's that tough-guy image that got people," Hank Jones says. "When Dale wasn't so hot on 'The Intimidator,' I told him, 'You know, there's a lot worse names people call you.' Everybody paid attention to him. He was the epitome of everybody sitting in the stands. He was so basic, such an old boy. The people in the stands . . . they were Dale."

America, it seemed, was ready for an Intimidator. And Hank Jones was ready to serve one up on a special collectible platter.

The story started when the dock business failed in Myrtle Beach, South Carolina. There were partners who later seemed to be suspicious and there were clients who never paid their bills and one thing led to another and the red ink washed over the black ink and maybe building docks wasn't the greatest route to solvency, after all. Hank Jones found himself broke.

What next? He still had entrepreneurial dreams and a growing family to feed and wanderlust in his mind. He basically took a pin and stuck it into a map of the South to find his next stop. The pin landed in Gaitlinburg, Tennessee.

"I just moved my family to Gaitlinburg," Jones says. "We had six people living in a thirty-eight-foot trailer. Want to get to know each other? Put six people in a thirty-eight-foot trailer to live."

Gaitlinburg was a tourist destination, the gateway to the Great Smoky Mountain National Park. Jones thought he could sell something to the tourists. A dropout after the sixth grade from the Orangeburg, South Carolina, school system, he always said his two basic assets were his mouth and his ability to do hard work. He could talk to people and make them interested. He could sell.

For this new venture, he bought an engraving machine and a bunch of sunglasses. What the tourist world needed—whether the tourist world knew it or not—was engraved sunglasses. And he had 'em.

"I started out on a street corner," he says. "People told me I was crazy. Six months later, I had a store."

Through the engraved-sunglass business, he met a man who knew a man who knew Conway Twitty, the country singer. Twitty was starting up his own amusement park, Twitty City. Hank Jones wound up as part of the Twitty City operation, commuting from Gaitlinburg, where his family kept the engraved-sunglasses business rolling. Twitty City led to NASCAR.

"This was around 1979, 1980," Jones says. "I always liked auto racing. I figured I could sell some sunglasses at the races on weekends. I brought the machine and the sunglasses to different races and set up outside the track."

The souvenir business was rudimentary, at best, at this NASCAR time. Darrell Waltrip remembers going to races with a box of T-shirts in the trunk of his car. That was his souvenir business. Richard Petty, himself, had just about gone broke pursuing the souvenir market. The mania simply hadn't hit.

"You know how you go to the track now and there are all those trailers out in front?" Jones says. "There was none of that. The tracks wouldn't let you come onto the grounds to sell. There weren't any trailers. I had this little kind of caboose that I pulled around. It was all small time. I was the one who brought out the first trailer for Bobby Allison, the 'Miller All-American Racing Team.'"

Set up in a field outside a track, Jones met Allison one weekend while selling sunglasses. Allsion simply stopped at the stand and started talking. The eventual result of the conversation was the trailer. The trailer was the start of everything.

"We had the trailer in 1984," Jones says. "Near the end of the season, Dale was talking to Bobby. They got talking about souvenirs. Dale said, 'I made $2,000 this year on souvenirs alone. How much did you make?' Bobby said, 'I made $25,000.' That's how I got to meet Dale. We talked, and at the end we had a deal. A handshake. That's all it was. For a lot of years, that was the only contract between us, that handshake."

The Dale Earnhardt souvenir trailer was on the road. Jones estimates that in the first season, 1985, Dale took home "about $180,000."

———

"It was so much different then," Jones says. "The people at the race-tracks didn't even want to talk to you. The first track that let us in was Martinsville. I paid the guy $500 for the weekend. It was a fight every-where. I was in Atlanta one time, setting up my trailer in a cow pasture across from the track. This old boy in blue jeans came by, driving his tractor, plowing the field. He asked why I wasn't setting up inside the track.

"I told him I'd tried, 'but this no-good son of a gun, Walt Nichols, president of the track,' wouldn't even meet with me, wouldn't even return my calls. Don't you know, the old boy in blue jeans smiled? He said, 'Well, I'm Walt Nichols, the no-good son of a gun, and I'll meet with you right now.' And that's how we got into Atlanta.

"Now they have fifty-five to sixty trailers at every race. For each trailer, it costs $9,500 just to pull up at Atlanta. It's a big business."

The fun was finding this market that never had existed. When Earn-hardt won that second championship in '86, then just dominated—through Intimidation, of course—the '87 season, the market grew and grew. With Goodwrench and the black car entering the picture in '87, the image was complete. Man in Black. No. 3. The Intimidator.

The great general boom time of athletic apparel had started. The gang kids were wearing satin Oakland Raiders jackets and Georgetown Hoyas baseball caps, and the trend was reaching out across the country. Nike was king. Reebok was close behind. Starter, the clothing company, was a major player. Look like the pros! Yes, people wanted to do that. NASCAR drivers were the pros, too.

"I didn't know what to call my company," Jones says. "I was fishing with Dale. I said I was either going to call it 'Racing Image' or 'Sports Image.' I asked what one he liked. We couldn't decide. Finally, he pulled a quarter from his pocket and flipped. Sports Image was the winner. So that was it."

For fun, Jones also became part of the Flying Aces pit crew for the No. 3 car. His job was to clean the windshield whenever Earnhardt came into the pits. He learned quickly that Earnhardt basically drove the entire race looking through a six-inch square in the lower half of the windshield. Jones learned by forgetting to clean that square one time.

"Dale starts pointing at that square," Jones says. "I saw him, but I pretended to ignore him. He starts really pointing. I kept ignoring him. Finally, the pit stop is about over and he's pointing, and pointing and just before he takes off, I clean the spot. After the race, we laughed about it and it became our thing. I never cleaned that spot until last. He'd always start pointing—every pit stop—and finally, I'd clean the spot.

"He could be tough—ask anyone who ever worked in the pits for him and he'll tell you the same thing—and he could make you mad. But when Dale went onto the track, you'd watch him drive that car the way he did and you'd just want to kiss him on the lips."

Sell his souvenirs and you also wanted to kiss him. Bubble-gum cards. Die-cast cars. Key chains. Bumper stickers. Playing cards. Lighters. Pendants. Buttons. Hats. Shirts and more shirts. Once set free, a river of merchandise rose higher and higher with each succeeding season. The tracks opened their gates, one by one. The other racing teams and drivers began showing up with their own trailers. The Earnhardt trailer was still the attraction.

The crowds would be larger at his trailer than at all of the other trailers combined. Jones eventually would add a second trailer, a third, fourth, and, for a while, a fifth. The demand always seemed to outstrip the supply . . . both the legal supply and the illegal supply.

"I spent all kinds of time running after the counterfeiters," Jones says. "I'd just want to grab 'em and lay 'em out. Dale, in fact, would tell me to calm down. I'd get hot.

"We spent a lot of money on lawyers' fees, getting trademarks for his signature, for the No. 3 car, for everything. There were very few trademarks at the time. We trademarked everything. General Motors didn't even have a trademark for 'Goodwrench.' We trademarked that. My idea was control. I wanted us to control everything that touched Dale."

Earnhardt and Teresa were involved in most decisions. Teresa had become his most valued business associate. There was a story that she had read all of the contracts her husband had ever signed, taken out the best, most favorable clauses in each of them, and made a new contract that included only these favorable clauses. This was the Dale Earnhardt contract, take it or leave it.

Jones remembers Teresa would argue for taste and decorum, the higher-quality item against the mass-market cheapie. Dale would agree. Jones remembers thinking how well Dale and Teresa worked together, partners and in love. They had the best situation.

"Dale Earnhardt listened to his wife and loved his wife," Jones says. "You always knew that."

The arrival of big money, though, brought pressures on the handshake business operation. As Earnhardt kept winning championships, four in the first five years of the nineties, and as sales and sponsorship deals grew and grew, as NASCAR grew, evolving into the dominant auto racing circuit in America, a new set of businessmen appeared wearing suits and ties and carrying expensive briefcases.

Jones had put Earnhardt merchandise into more than 10,000 Goodwrench service departments around the country, an instant network of stores. That was big money. The Earnhardt catalog listed almost 800 different items. More big money. The size of the Earnhardt market was shown by a visit by Jones and Earnhardt to QVC, the television shopping network. In two hours, almost a million dollars was spent on Intimidator merchandise. All of the network's 2,800 phone lines were busy at one time with 1,300 callers on hold, waiting.

The guy with the sixth-grade education began feeling hemmed in, surrounded, by the new MBAs and money merchants. Everything was much more serious.

"I was running around. . . . I think about it and thank God I got out," Hank Jones says. "I'd be dead by now, the way I was going. People were just coming at Dale from all directions. I didn't want to share anything.

That was my idea. Looking back, I probably was wrong to think the way I did, probably tried to hang on too long, but that was just the way I was at the time."

The 1994 season was the time of change. Neil Bonnett had died in February and Earnhardt had swallowed his grief, the way he always did, working it out internally. The sadness never showed, but Jones thinks it made Earnhardt look at life differently.

"Neil was that once-in-a-lifetime buddy," Jones says. "Those two guys had a special charisma between them. I think Neil's death made Dale realize that nothing lasts forever, that he had to take stock and put things together. I don't know what financial situation Neil was in when he died, but I think Dale thought about that."

The money was more serious and Earnhardt was more serious. He bought his first piece of the property in Mooresville, the start of a 900-acre empire that would include his new house (the family would move from the house on Lake Norman that Rod Osterlund encouraged him to buy) and his two-story, 108,000-square-foot corporate headquarters that would be so flashy it would be called the "Garage Mahal."

Earnhardt had added a business manager, Don Hawk, toward the end of the '93 season. That was how much the game had changed. A minister and former car salesman, Hawk became Earnhardt's controversial business face. Jones didn't like the face.

"From day one, Don Hawk was out to remove Dale from all the people who'd been around him," Hank Jones says. "It was all 'This guy's cheating you' and 'That guy's cheating you,' and the truth was no one was cheating him. The guy was just a good bullshitter. He tried to get my partner, Joey Tilman, to back-door me and then, when I found out, he tried to get me to back-door Joey Tilman.

"Put all this in the book, because this isn't anything I haven't said to Don Hawk's face. I wish him all the very worst in life."

Under pressure, Jones wound up selling Sports Image to Earnhardt.

Sports Image wound up being folded into a new company, Action Performance, which controls much of the NASCAR souvenir business today. Earnhardt came out with a chunk of Action Performance stock.

Jones says he was hurt when the transaction took place, "because I confused friendship with business." He says he has sorted that all out now and that Earnhardt was, indeed, a friend. Business simply was business. The Intimidator business had grown far beyond engraving sunglasses.

"I still have the machine," Jones says. "I still have a dream of showing it off in a glass case in the lobby of some company headquarters of mine. I'm fifty-seven years old and still have dreams."

He now sells souvenirs for Terry Labonte and a half dozen NASCAR stars. His people park the trailers inside the gates.

The change in Earnhardt through all this was noticeable. The guy who once would blow off sponsor events to go fishing and hunting with Bonnett would now appear at the events to shake the hands and make the small talk. The prime NASCAR movers—Bill France Jr. and T. Wayne Robertson, head of sports marketing at R. J. Reynolds, were two examples—always had preached the virtues of image to the sport's biggest star, and now the words seemed to have taken hold.

The game seemed to matter more. Money was another competition.

"I think it's safe to say he looked at those stats in Street and Smith's or wherever they were published, the rankings of which athletes made how much money," Jeff Byrd, president of Bristol Raceway, formerly with R. J. Reynolds, says. "I'm sure he knew where he ranked against Michael Jordan and Tiger Woods. This was just another race he was in.

"When he started out, he could care less about cocktail parties and schmoozing. I don't think the man ever changed, but he certainly became more of a businessman. He controlled an empire, making 30 to

40 million dollars a year and he lived that lifes... houses, the ranches, the corporation with 300 to 400 ... doesn't change the man, but it changes the way he opera... processes.

"I think it was, 'We not only beat 'em on the race track, we ... in the boardroom, too.' Dale was a pretty savvy guy."

The toys became larger and larger. The ATVs and trucks were joineL by a Learjet, by three King Air turboprops, by a helicopter. Home on the road became a giant trailer, pulled out to three times its normal size, all the comforts of modern living. ("I think Dale was one of the first drivers to have a trailer," Hank Jones says. "I had one before him. He used to come there before races. Before he had the trailer, he'd be sitting in the hauler with fifteen guys before the race began. I'd bring him to my trailer, just so he could get away.") He had a seventy-five-foot boat, *Sunday Money,* complete with captain and crew.

The image of midlife success fully eclipsed the image of the wild-eyed country boy. Hawk sold Earnhardt as an athlete more than a successful stock car racer. "The Michael Jordan of motor sports." This was a man who finished off a good bowl of endorsed Wheaties with an endorsed Coke and maybe an endorsed Oreo cookie for dessert. Check him out, America. Be like Dale.

"Don obviously enjoys what he's doing and gets extremely excited when asked to compare his man against some of the biggest names in sports merchandising—Michael Jordan of the Chicago Bulls, Shaquille O'Neal of the Los Angeles Lakers, Emmitt Smith and Troy Aikman of the Dallas Cowboys," Jerome Lucido wrote in a 1998 biography of Don Hawk, titled *Racing with the Hawk: The Man Behind Dale Earnhardt.* "Don believes that Earnhardt's visibility and popularity are increasing at such a rate that he'll soon be up there with any of these sports figures, and perhaps be able to beat them out in competition for marketing dollars."

There was a certain poetic beauty to this new picture, the total trih over hard times, hard beginnings, but there also was a certain kwardness to it. How much had been lost in the refining of Dale arnhardt? Humpy Wheeler remembers going to some event where Earnhardt was wearing a tailored blue suit.

"It was from a certain tailor in Charlotte who sells to all the big executives in the city and it looked great, but at the same time it kind of bothered me a little bit," Wheeler says. "I said to myself, 'Who's doing this to him?' There were all kinds of forces working on him. Here's this huge amount of money coming in and he's got to do something with it. What do you do? The pull of time became so much. He always had to be somewhere. He had that boat in Florida with the full-time captain, the mate, and how many days a year could he be there? Ten? Fourteen? The pull of time was everywhere."

There was a business deal that also bothered Wheeler. His track was trying to purchase an adjacent 120 acres for parking. The seller was balking at the track's offer. Wheeler thought negotiations were continuing, then suddenly found the piece of land had been sold. And Earnhardt was one of the buyers. And Earnhardt hadn't said a thing to Wheeler. And Wheeler blew up. What kind of friendship was this?

"Dale eventually called—he knew I was mad—and said, 'I want to come and see you,'" Wheeler says. "We talked for two hours and he said 'I don't want this to come between us' and it didn't. But it was something different from him than what I had expected."

Jeff Byrd remembers his worst argument with Earnhardt. Byrd says Earnhardt had "the best smile you've ever seen and the worst stare you've ever seen." The stare came into effect when Byrd was working for R. J. Reynolds. Earnhardt objected to his picture being on a calendar put out by Winston cigarettes, because Winston had not paid a rights fee. Byrd told Earnhardt to check the small print on the contract that every driver in Winston Cup has to sign before being allowed to race. The driver's likeness may be used by Winston for promotional purposes. End of argument.

"Dale just stared at me for about forty-five seconds, then turned around and left the room," Byrd says. "The next time I saw him, though, it was like it never happened."

In February of 1995, Ed Hinton wrote a long profile of the new-look Earnhardt for *Sports Illustrated*. It wasn't a particularly flattering profile and brought about the end to a long relationship between the driver and writer. Earnhardt was depicted, sitting in a room, signing autographs at a machine-shop pace—but only autographs on "authorized" bubble-gum cards—while Hawk made deals in the background. The revenue from souvenir sales in 1994 was "estimated" at $50 million. Earnhardt's personal income had been estimated at $5.5 million, but Hinton said the figure was closer to $14 million. Earnhardt was quoted as saying his situation "sometimes seems like a runaway train," adding, "I don't have time for family life."

Hinton asked if Earnhardt even felt like the same person anymore.

"Sometimes I do," Earnhardt replied. "Sometimes you wonder. It is unnnnnn-believable, though."

———

The businesses of Dale Earnhardt would continue to grow. In 2000, Forbes would rank him 40th in its list of the 100 Richest Celebrities. His income would be conservatively estimated at $24.5 million and he would be listed between talk-show hostess Rosie O'Donnell (39) and the rock group Kiss (41).

Hawk would be dropped from the operation, basically replaced by Teresa, who would run the company. The idea of Earnhardt as multimillionaire and businessman would be accepted much better, both by other people and himself. The newness would be gone for everyone. He would grow into the image of family man, successful man, still the rascal on the track, everything tied together in a grand package. Happiness would come back into his life from an unexpected direction, the rise of his son as a race car driver.

It all would simply take time. And a win at Daytona wouldn't hurt, either.

"It all works out," Hank Jones says. "Life goes on. I still went hunting and fishing with Dale. We were fine. I have a couple of cases of everything we ever made. I suppose they're worth a few million dollars right now, the way things have gone. I won't sell any of them, though. They're going to charities for auction. I think Dale would be smiling at me for handling it that way. I would hope so."

8

AT THE ALTAR

The fans forced the memorial services. The fans just called. The fans just showed up. There wasn't a plan at most of the tracks in the country to hold any special service, but the fans demanded one. The fans needed one.

"We've got to do something," Jeff Byrd, president of Bristol Motor Speedway, told Wayne Estes, his vice president for communications. "The switchboards are going crazy. The e-mails keep coming. People need a place to go."

Every track contained its own shared memories between the fan and the man. Bristol was where Dale Earnhardt won his first race. Bristol was where he bumped Terry Labonte out of the way. Bristol was where he showed up once and helped build the track, itself.

"We were doing our first major addition," Byrd says. "It was looking like we weren't going to make it in time for the season. The guys

were working a stretch of eighty-six ten-hour days in a row. They were just beat. Couldn't help it.

"I was on the phone with Dale for some reason and I told him about our problems. He said, right away, 'Well, maybe I should come up there and get those guys going.' He flew up a couple of days later, talked with everybody. All these guys who were driving the bulldozers, hanging the steel, the construction guys. They just loved it. He was one of them. The next day . . . it was like the first day on the job all over again. Everybody was flying. We were ready for the season."

A wall was put up before the service, a place for people to write out messages. The service was held, Estes giving a speech. The crowd was estimated at between 5,000 and 6,000 people. A reporter from the local newspaper said she never would forget the prevailing smell of the day: flowers and cigarette smoke. . . .

DAYTONA

Larry McReynolds was new to the operation. He was the latest crew chief for Richard Childress Racing, and the Daytona 500 was his first race for the team in 1997. He didn't know how to act. The stakes had changed dramatically. He was at Daytona, and now he was with Dale Earnhardt.

"The Daytona 500 is strange anyway," he says. "You're going to the Super Bowl to start the season instead of finish it. Most of your energy, most of your testing in the off-season, is toward Daytona. There's always some big unknown, some new car or technology change, on the scene. You get down to Speed Week and until the last hour of the last day you're always trying to make the car better."

The special buzz of the Daytona day, sort of like Christmas with pit stops, everything new and exciting and unexpected, was heightened by being with Earnhardt. Earnhardt's history at Daytona brought a buzz on top of the buzz. Here was the great racer, the seven-time champion, who somehow never had won the greatest jewel in his sport. Zero for 18. Nada. He was Ahab and Daytona was his fat, white, 0-for-18, concrete-walled whale.

McReynolds, highly respected after ten years with Robert Yates racing, part of Daytona wins in 1991 with Davey Allison and 1996 with Dale Jarrett, had been plugged into the saga with great fanfare in the off-season. Andy Petree had left after the two championships and a second-place finish in '95 to start his own race team, and his replacements hadn't worked magic. McReynolds was supposed to be the answer. He was optimistic about his new job.

"It was time for me to make a move," he says. "I'd been running two cars at Robert Yates and felt I was stretched too much. There's only so much you can do. When Richard called, it just made sense to me."

If anyone knew the ups and downs of the sport, McReynolds did. ("The Good Lord throws a lot of curveballs in this game," he says.) He'd worked with Davey Allison, better and better every year, until Davey died in the helicopter crash in '94 at Talladega. Davey had been replaced in the car by Ernie Irvan, who also had done better and better and then been sidelined by a wicked crash in Michigan. Who could ever tell what would come next?

Irvan had been back in form in '96 and Jarrett had been solid in the other Yates car, a combined six wins, three poles, and two top ten finishers in the points standings. There was promise with Robert Yates, but McReynolds felt there was more promise with Childress and Earnhardt.

"I said, right away, 'Gosh, what a deal,'" McReynolds says. "I'd be working with the best driver in the sport, and if things worked out even half as well as I thought they could, we'd be like a snowball coming through that nobody'd ever seen."

The Daytona 500 seemed to be the start of that snowball. The car was working great. The driver was working great. On Thursday, Earnhardt had proclaimed, "I feel like I'm bulletproof." He seemed to be right. Everything was working to perfection as the race progressed. Twenty laps to go, Earnhardt was in the lead. McReynolds felt excited as he saw the black car come past with each circuit of the track. This was when he didn't know how to act.

He looked around the Childress pit but didn't see the same excitement. He saw edginess. OK, he knew the history. OK, OK. Should he say anything? Should he stay silent? The excitement finally won the battle.

"Looks good, huh?" he said to Childress.

"I've been here too many times," Childress replied.

"Sure enough," McReynolds says. "Eleven laps to go? We were upside down on the backstretch."

How'd it happen this time? Just another doozie to add to a long string of doozies. Earnhardt was running second, waiting to make his move. Jeff Gordon, who eventually won the race, saw Earnhardt drift high toward the wall and saw an opening. Earnhardt drifted back down, hit Gordon in the door, and went flying. He was upside down. He was banging off Ernie Irvan. He was spinning.

When the mangled car finally stopped its wayward course, Earnhardt emerged and went to the ambulance. He was about to go to the track hospital when he looked back at the car and said, "Man, the wheels ain't knocked off that car yet." Could it still run? He ran toward the driver of the wrecker as if the car were being towed from Cannon Boulevard in Kannapolis for being double-parked. Wait. Stop.

He was back in the car. The car could go! He was back on the track, driving home a wrecked No. 3 for a 31st-place finish.

Larry McReynolds, waiting in the pits, excitement gone, finally understood. He, too, was now living with the streak that seemed as if it never would end.

This was Dale Earnhardt at Daytona.

———————

How do these streaks begin? When does someone in the press box, some scorekeeper for public opinion, look at the record of individual losses in individual events, separate events in different years, and notice a trend? When does that whisper start? *He can't win the big one. Pass it on.* There are streaks in all sports, curses of the Bambino in Boston, missed field goals by kickers from Buffalo, Phil Mickelson in yet another bunker at yet another big moment, great players left without championship rings, Elizabeth Taylor divorced yet again. Is this random circumstance? A pattern that feeds on itself? What?

All the athlete knows—"No, there's no such thing as a curse," he invariably says. "No, of course not"—is that he is in a box. He doesn't think he made the box, but now it exists and until he climbs out of it he is doomed to hear the whispers. Earnhardt was in the box of boxes.

Here was Daytona, the greatest race in his sport, no doubt about that, the foundation of the sport, starting with those legendary races on the flat and hard beaches, and here he was, arguably the greatest racer in his sport, and he couldn't win the damn thing. Name a way to lose and he'd done it. He'd cut a tire at the end, run out of gas, been passed on the last lap, finished far back in the field. There didn't seem to be many other plots available.

It wasn't as if he couldn't handle the track. It wasn't as if he didn't love the track. He'd won more other races at Daytona, 29, than any other driver in history. When he came into the 1997 race, he'd won the Pepsi 400, the other Daytona race, twice, had won a Twin 125 qualifying race for the past seven straight years, had finished second in the Daytona 500, itself, in three of the past four years.

The race, the track, was some lovely tease. He simply couldn't close the deal. He'd been going there since 1975, back in those no-money days, when he showed up for the first time with three friends to drive in a Sportsman's race. He'd loved the place from the start. First time he saw it, he thought he had arrived at an automotive Oz.

"We drove down here, I was driving a one-ton truck, pulling the trailer and race car, and all our stuff was throwed into the back of it," he told Godwin Kelly of the *Daytona News-Journal.* "It was my dad's old truck. We come off onto Highway 92. You could see the grandstand from a great distance away. We go to the track and you're just driving along and you keep driving along. You go through one light, two lights, and another light and you're still driving by the Speedway. It was pretty damn amazing just seeing it from the outside by a kid who has just seen half miles and quarter miles [tracks].

"When we got checked in and got inside the track, they parked us out back. I looked around and I said, 'What is this?' I saw all these big turns. I knew it was Daytona, but I couldn't have imagined it was this big. It was pretty interesting and exciting and intimidating when I first came in the place and seen it. When I first went out to practice, I was like, 'Damn, where do I run on this thing? Up high? Down low?' You could run just about anywhere you wanted because you'd run flat out.

"I've had some great wins here, some great experiences. I've had some tragic experiences, like losing Neil . . . I've had some bad crashes here. Still, it's the track I would choose to race at any given day."

How had all this stuff happened?

This was his Daytona 500 history:

1979—Eighth. One lap down. A rookie. Started 10th.
1980—Fourth. Led on seven different occasions after starting 32nd.
    Still close at end.
1981—Fifth.

1982—Thirty-sixth. Completed only 44 of the 200 laps before Bud
   Moore's Ford failed.

1983—Thirty-fifth. Ditto. Completed only 63 of the 200 laps.

1984—Second. Couldn't get past Cale Yarborough.

1985—Thirty-second. Engine failure, 84 laps.

1986—Thirteenth. Fighting eventual winner Geoff Bodine for the
   lead, his car ran out of fuel with three laps to go.

1987—Fifth. Not a strong contender.

1988—Tenth. Ditto.

1989—Third. Close, but lost to Darrell Waltrip in the pits with 10 laps
   left.

1990—Fifth. The true start of jinx talk. Was leading the race, going to
   win, as he took the white flag for the final lap. More than halfway
   through the lap, one mile to go, two turns, his right rear tire was
   cut and began to fall apart. Unknown Derrike Cope drops low past
   Earnhardt as his car fades right. Flat tire. Broken heart.

1991—Fifth. Was at the front of the field with two laps left. Bumped
   with Davey Allison and spun.

1992—Ninth. Crashed.

1993—Second. Passed by Dale Jarrett on the last lap.

1994—Seventh. Not in contention.

1995—Second. Late charge at winner Sterling Marlin falls short.

1996—Second. Jarrett again. Couldn't get past on last lap.

1997—Thirty-first. The crash with Gordon. The battered car going
   around the track. The same, same thing.

Nineteen years. It was an incredible list of frustration. (Monday,
banged thumb with hammer. Tuesday, fell off ladder. Wednesday. . . .)
The ripped-apart back tire from '90 was mounted on a piece of oak like
a trophy and still hung from a wall in Richard Childress's shop. It was
the only Daytona 500 trophy the team or Earnhardt had.

Earnhardt said, "You could write a big book on everything that's happened to me the last nineteen years in the Daytona 500." A very big book. A saga.

The twentieth chapter had arrived.

There were added questions about Earnhardt when he checked into Daytona for the 1998 500. The old *can't win the big one* had been replaced by *can't win any one*. Was he done? The snowball that McReynolds had anticpated when he joined Childress Racing had never developed. There could be no snowball without any snow. For the first time since 1981, Earnhardt had gone winless for the entire season in '97. He had a streak now of 56 races without a win. There were reports that he and McReynolds were feuding.

"We just had different philosophies on a lot of things," McReynolds says. "Like qualifying. He didn't think much of qualifying, said it didn't matter much where you started. I thought qualifying was another race and you should go out and try to win it. Things like that."

Earnhardt was forty-six years old, two months shy of forty-seven. He was old for an athlete. While race car drivers usually start later and compete longer than most athletes, he also was getting old for a race car driver. He thought Richard Petty had retired late at fifty-five. He thought A. J. Foyt had retired late at fifty-nine. He didn't have to look any further than his old rival, Darrell Waltrip, still driving at fifty-one, but in the middle of the pack, stroking, to see what he didn't want to do. Then again, he told everyone he felt good. He certainly didn't want to quit.

"It's been a long time since we've won, and it will be nice to win again," he said at one time during the streak. "I want the fans booing me like they used to. And I still think we will win that eighth champ-ionship."

A reporter asked if that was realistic. The reporter received the stare.

"You be leading the race on the last lap and let me be behind you and see," Earnhardt finally said. "When drivers get older, they get smarter. They don't forget anything they've ever done. I don't. So I would hate to have me behind me on the last lap and I hadn't won a race all year and his bumper could get to me."

There still were doubts. Humpy Wheeler, the old friend at Lowe's Speedway, was one of the doubters. He still has doubts.

"I don't think anyone should be in a race car over forty-five, certainly over fifty," he says. "Maybe NASCAR should do something about that. Your body changes when you get older. Your reflexes aren't the same. Your brain shrinks. You just don't react the same. You don't."

Two disquieting moments had occurred in the past two seasons as possible proofs to Wheeler's theory. The first was a tumultuous crash at Talladega in '96. The second was a strange blackout at Darlington in '97. It sometimes seemed as if Earnhardt's body was telling him this was the time to leave.

"The crash at Talladega was about the worst crash you can imagine without someone getting killed," Wheeler says. "Most drivers can't remember the crashes. They get knocked out. Dale remembered every bit of that crash. He was on his side and in the middle of the track and he could see the other cars come along and hit him. What do you think it's like to be in something like that?

"Drivers come away with one of two thoughts after a bad crash. One is 'Gosh, another inch or two and I would be dead.' The second is 'If I can survive that, I can survive anything.' Which of the two thoughts you have determines how you're going to be as a driver for the rest of your career."

"He dodged a cannonball out there," Tim Brewer, crew chief for driver John Andretti, said at the time. "He didn't dodge a bullet, he dodged a cannonball."

The crash was on the tri-oval at Talladega, the fastest part of the track. Earnhardt was leading on the 117th lap. A knot of cars was following. The eventual result left him with a broken sternum, broken collarbone, and bruised pelvis. He described the events better than anyone else at a press conference the next week in Indianapolis. This might have been the most involved, most detailed, most graphic accident report ever filed by anyone involved in any accident in any car, even the family sedan:

"When I came through the tri-oval, I knew the 4 car [Sterling Marlin] was on my right rear," he said. "I knew the 28 [Ernie Irvan] was right behind me. The last glance I saw of the 28, he was on the inside of my left rear. Then the car turned abruptly to the right.

"When the car turned abruptly sideways, I knew I was going to hit the wall. When it hit the wall is when I broke my sternum. When the car got on the side and got up in the air a little bit, it was spinning around. I seen a flash and another car hit me at the same time. It was probably Derrike [Cope]. There was a big crash and the car went airborne again. That's when I broke my collarbone and bruised my pelvis.

"It stayed on the left side of the car for a long time. A lot of fire and sparks were coming in the car at that point. I could see the asphalt. The 33 [Robert Pressley] hit, and that's when it pushed the top and dash down in the car. It also pushed the carburetor and air cleaner and everything down into the engine.

"The car sat back down on the ground and on its wheels, spinning around. The 29 car [Greg Sacks] went by on my left, and then a red car hit the front end. I assumed at that point—from the replay I couldn't tell much—it was either Ken Schrader or the 94 [Bill Elliott]. Come to find out, it was Schrader. He said, 'I seen you and I aimed for you.'

"I held on to the steering wheel practically the whole time. I was bouncing around the car, but I was still braced in there pretty good. The car stopped and the smoke was running out from under the dash because the wires were burning because the dash was knocked down into the car. I switched the battery switch off and I started trying to unbuckle my helmet. I knew my collarbone was hurt.

"About the same time, the safety crews and [NASCAR's] Steve

Peterson and Buster Auton got to me. I told 'em not to cut the top off because I thought I could get out. They worked with me and pulled me out of the car.

"I wanted to lay down. I didn't want to stand up, but I had to because it hurt too bad to lay down, so I said, 'Just walk me to the ambulance.' That's why I was walking instead of laying on the stretcher. I didn't want to walk."

When he had arrived at Talladega, he was back in the championship hunt after a down year in '95. He'd won two races and was 12 points behind Terry Labonte for the Winston Cup lead. When he left Talladega in the ambulance, his championship possibilities were gone. Even though he wore a flak jacket and gritted his teeth and qualified at Indy and started the race the next weekend and even though he ran Watkins Glen a week after that, he clearly was still hurting. He was finished for the rest of the year and finished fourth in the points race.

The second disquieting moment, the blackout at Darlington, was simply bizarre. Earnhardt fell asleep on the parade laps. Or passed out. Or . . . something. He looked as if he were involved in the first DUI situation in NASCAR history. The doctors never did clearly discover what was wrong.

There didn't seem to be anything different when he pulled his chair under an umbrella during the drivers' meeting in the South Carolina heat ("The rest of us were wondering why we didn't do it, too," Jeff Gordon said), and there wasn't even any concern when he fell asleep in the car on the starting grid. He had been known to do that. The worry began when the command "Start your engines" was given and he had to be awakened again.

Never a big talker on the two-way radio, there nevertheless were things he was supposed to say as the cars came up to speed. He did not say them. The only time he talked, answering only one question on the three parade laps, his voice was slurred. When the rest of the field started to take off at the first turn toward the starting line, Earnhardt fell behind and then ran into the wall. He then drove the length of the track and crashed harder into the wall at the second turn.

With Richard Childress yelling into the radio, "Dale, park the car," he missed the entrance to pit road the first time, then made it the second time. After saying, "I'm sorry, I saw two racetracks," he was taken to the infield care center, then to a hospital in Florence, South Carolina.

Eventually, five doctors, three hospitals, and countless tests proved inconclusive. Was this the start of heart problems? It suddenly was pointed out that Earnhardt now, at forty-six, was a year older than his father, Ralph, had been when he died. The tests all said his heart was fine. Earnhardt always claimed that he passed out from eating a fresh tomato, drinking two sport drinks, and taking three muscle relaxers before the race. He, like his doctors, said he was fine, good as ever.

Except he wasn't winning races anymore.

———

The days preceding the 1998 Daytona 500 also were not wonderful for Earnhardt. True, he won a Twin 125 race, but this was the ninth straight year he'd won a Twin 125 race. A win in the Twin 125 was not exactly a positive omen. The more important thing was that he came down with a head cold on Thursday and skipped the morning practice on Friday and the afternoon practice, then was rained out, and then on Saturday . . .

"We had a glitch," Larry McReynolds says. "An engine problem. We had to put in a new engine Saturday night."

If he was bothered, though, Earnhardt never showed it. He was bulletproof, remember? He had watched the Denver Broncos and John Elway win the Super Bowl in January, climbing out of their own little can't-win-the-big-one box, and that was his hook.

"See that look in my eyes?" he told everyone. "That's the same look John Elway had at the Super Bowl."

Any developing thoughts of depression were put away on Saturday afternoon. Walking back from practice—thinking about the blown engine, the troubles—he ran into Lesa France Kennedy, Bill France Jr.'s daughter. She asked him if he would come to meet a group of Make-a-Wish children, kids who had severe physical problems. He agreed.

"So I went into this little office and sat down with these three kids, two boys and one little girl," he later explained. "And they were just all big smiles and big No. 3 hats and everything, got autographs and everything. And the little girl . . . she gave me a penny and she said, 'Dale, this is your good-luck penny. You're going to win the race.' And, I don't know, something about that just felt good. To see that little girl with all her problems in life . . . she's in a wheelchair, she's probably eight years old. Life hasn't dealt her a good hand at all, and she was all excited, being at Daytona and meeting her favorite race car driver.

"So we took that penny and glued it on the dashboard. Richard and the guys changed the engine in that race car and tuned it and we went out and won the Daytona 500. And it just felt like it was going to happen. Whether anybody that raced me all day long was behind me or ahead of me, wherever, it didn't seem to be a worry. It was just our day. It was just our time."

The race unfolded as so many Daytona 500s had for him. He was in the mix all the way, one of the leaders. Jeff Gordon also looked strong early, but hit a piece of debris on lap 123 and his car became hard to handle. Wait . . . piece of debris? Shouldn't that have been Earnhardt? Not this time.

He led once, twice, three times, four, and on the 140th of the 200 laps went around Childress teammate Mike Skinner to move into the lead for the fifth and final time. There would be heat behind him, Ford teammates Jeremy Mayfield and Rusty Wallace in pursuit, joined by

Bobby Labonte, but this time he was free of the trouble, able to block all moves. When John Andretti and Robert Pressley collided somewhere behind him, bringing out a yellow caution flag at the same time as the white final-lap flag, the race was won.

Or was it?

Dale Earnhardt drove probably the fastest caution lap in Daytona history to win the race. He started the lap slowly, but then put his foot to the gas. Just in case. Just to make sure. You know?

The crowd of more than 175,000 people stood and cheered as if it had seen the removal of a giant impacted wisdom tooth. The crews and drivers from virtually every other team stood in a chain on pit row to extend high-fives and congratulations, a gauntlet of appreciation. The man of the hour—maybe he cried, no, maybe his eyes just watered up, not real crying, no—drove onto the painted grass logo in front of the grandstand and executed a pair of perfect doughnuts that left a tire mark of a perfect "3." He autographed the track!

"I'm pretty good at writin', huh?" he asked.

All the frustrations came out of him when he walked into the press conference in the press box and threw a stuffed monkey across the room. Yes, the monkey was off his back. He never had made any pretenses about not wanting to win the race, never had tried to downplay it. Yes, this was the one. This was the one that always had gotten away. This was the one he had. Finally.

"The years of disappointment, the close calls, all the chapters have been written," he said. "Now the 20th chapter is in. To win this race is something you can't, I mean you really can't, put into words. You can talk about it all day, but you can't put into words the feelings you have inside. It's everything you've ever worked hard to do, and you've finally accomplished it. It's just pretty damn impressive, especially with everything we've done here in the past and all the shortcomings we've had in this race."

He waved to the fans who were scooping up the sod where he had made his autograph with the car. The fans formed themselves into an unruly and slightly inebriated No. 3 and waved back. He hugged Teresa and Richard Childress and any friend available. He exulted—not too strong a word to use—exulted. His day. His time.

"I was working for a Charlotte TV station," John Roberts from Fox says. "We were doing a live shot maybe two hours after the race ended. The track was empty. I'm standing, waiting to begin, and here comes Earnhardt. He's driving a little golf cart and he has the biggest bottle of champagne I ever have seen.

"I decided to take a shot and yelled, 'Dale, want to come on and talk to the people back in Kannapolis?' He stopped the cart and asked when we were on. I told him, 'Five minutes,' and he jumped in the cart and said, 'I'll be back.' I said to myself, 'OK, that's the end of him.' Five minutes later, though, there he was. And he had Childress with him.

"He was still flying."

The win was his final shove into mainstream American culture. The people who knew nothing and cared less about fast automobiles flying around the track were charmed by the sight of this middle-aged gent conquering a personal Everest, smiling and—yes—exulting. This was pretty good stuff. Hey, take a look at this guy, Martha.

This was his mainstream breakout moment. Question: Race car driver? Answer: Dale Earnhardt. There was no doubt anymore. He had moved into the true A list of celebrity. Everybody wanted him. Seven Winston Cup championships might have shown how good he was at what he did, but the Daytona 500 moved him in with the biggest rock stars, the Hollywood icons, the Michael Jordans of the land. He was hot.

David Letterman called. . . .

Top Ten List:

Reasons It Took Me Twenty Years to Win the Daytona 500

(as read by Dale Earnhardt):

10. It took me nineteen years to realize I had the emergency brake on.

9. Finally rotated and balanced my mustache.

8. Quit training with the Canadian snowboarding team.

7. Stopped letting my 300-pound cousin, Ricky, ride shotgun.

6. New strategy: pretend I'm Dave driving home on the Merritt Parkway.

5. Who cares it took me twenty years—at least my name isn't Dick Trickle.

4. Just figured out that if you mash the gas pedal all the way down, the car takes off like an SOB.

3. My new pit crew—the Spice Girls.

2. This year, whenever I passed them, I gave them the finger.

1. My secret to success: one can of motor oil in my engine, one can of motor oil in my pants!

He appeared on *King of the Hill* as a cartoon character and in the movie *BASEketball* . . .

The businesses went crazy. . . .

He addressed the National Press Club in Washington. . . .

The National Press Club in Washington? That was the coolest one of all. The master of ceremonies was Doug Harbrecht, news editor of *Business Week* magazine. The luncheon was broadcast on CSPAN and National Public Radio.

"Before introducing our head table today, I would like to remind our members of some upcoming speakers," Harbrecht said in his introductory remarks. "This week Richard Holbrooke, chief negotiator for the Dayton Accord on Bosnia, will speak on Thursday. He is followed by Lionel Jospin, Prime Minister of France, on Friday. He will be discussing his visit to the United States and his talks with President Clinton. Our last speaker in June will be Jane Fonda on June 24.

"We also have quite a lineup for July. Michael Isikoff, investigative reporter for *Newsweek* magazine, will be speaking about breaking the Monica Lewinsky story on July 8. He is followed by Jerzy Buzek, the prime minister of Poland, on July 9. And the following week, we'll hear Phillippe deMontebello, director of the Metropolitan Museum of Art on July 14. He will speak about plundered art from the Holocaust. And finally in July, we will hear Senator Robert Bennett speak on July 15 about the Year 2000 computer programming problem and its effect on government systems. . . ."

And after that, after a proper introduction, the ragtag kid from Kannapolis, once unable to open his mouth in front of educated strangers, stood and addressed the Washington press corps. And did a damn good job, too. Maybe better than the prime minister of France. Maybe better than the prime minister of Poland. Maybe Jane Fonda, too.

9

AT THE ALTAR

Richard Sturtz doesn't really drive the truck a lot. He takes it to car shows. People see the decals on the side and the autograph of Dale Earnhardt across the dashboard and they want to talk. Richard Sturtz talks to them. He tells his story easily. There is magic in it.

"I always liked Dale Earnhardt," the forty-six-year-old mechanic from Mt. Savage, Maryland, begins. "I liked him for twenty-one years, from the start. I liked the way he was down to earth. I liked the way he sort of liked to bump people. He was my man."

Sturtz and his wife, Karen, would make an annual pilgrimage to the races at Lowe's in Charlotte. They rooted for Earnhardt. At one of the Winston booths, a staple at all races, little tents where the tobacco company hands out free cigarettes, Sturtz absentmindedly filled out an entry in the spring of 2000 for a contest called the Winston No Bull 5. He forgot all about the entry until a Federal Express package arrived a month later.

"What are you, bringing me a check?" he asked the driver as he signed the receipt of delivery.

Well, better than that. Sturtz was a finalist in the contest. He and Karen had an expense-paid trip to the Winston 500 in the fall at Talladega. They also had a chance to win a million bucks.

The format was sort of convoluted. Five fans had been chosen. Five drivers were eligible also to win a million. Each fan was paired with a driver. If the driver won the race, he won a million and the fan won another million.

Two days before the race, the fans and drivers were taken to a skeet-shooting range in Alpine, Alabama. The drivers shot skeet and then were matched, by the order of their finish, with the fans. Earnhardt finished fourth. Sturtz was listed fourth. Magic.

"You and Karen are going to go home with some money," Earnhardt promised. Money? Sturtz was happy enough to hear his hero speak. Money was secondary.

The race—Earnhardt's 76th and final NASCAR victory—couldn't have been more exciting. This was restrictor-plate action, close and terrifying and seemingly designed for the man in the black suit. Eighteenth with four laps to go, he weaved and battled and forced his way to the front and broke free. Richard Sturtz wound up standing on top of the Monte Carlo with The Intimidator, waving at the crowd in Victory Lane. Two millionaires.

"I told him right that day that a black Silverado Dale Earnhardt Chevrolet truck would look awfully good in my garage," Sturtz said. *"He tried to talk me out of it—tried to tell me to invest my money—but I knew what I wanted. Two weeks later, Karen and I picked up the truck at his dealership in Newton, North Carolina. He came over and took us back to his farm and we had lunch with his family and he acted like we'd known each other forever."*

Sturtz took some of the rest of his money and invested it in a garage. He had been a truck driver for most of his life, but now does what he *always wanted to do: fix cars. He says he is very happy in what he does, that he has fulfilled a dream. He tells people at the car shows, well, that Dale Earnhardt changed his life. . . .*

FULFILLMENT

In the summer of 1999, Earnhardt consented to do an interview with *Sports Illustrated* for the magazine's annual NASCAR preview edition for the 2000 season. The story angle was the debut of Dale Jr. on the Winston Cup circuit, the beginning of yet another father-son driving combination in the big show.

NASCAR always contained a strong streak of nepotism, with sons and brothers and second cousins and friends of famous drivers all moving onto the scene. The Earnhardts now had joined the crowd of Pettys and Jarretts and Labontes and Bodines and Waltrips and Burtons. Dale Jr., now twenty-four years old, in the midst of winning his second straight Busch championship, also was driving in five Winston events in '99 and would expand to the full schedule in 2000.

Negotiations for the interview took a while to complete, first because Earnhardt was in the midst of his usual busy whirl, flying here and there on his days off from the weekend racing, and second because he now hated Ed Hinton, who was the *SI* motor racing writer at the time. Once the best of friends, Earnhardt hadn't talked directly with Hinton since Hinton's 1995 *SI* story. The two men had exchanged questions and answers in press conference situations, the words touched by ice, but never had done a one-on-one interview. Earnhardt wasn't doing one-on-one interviews with anyone very often. He would do the *SI* interview only if Hinton weren't involved.

"To tell the truth, I'll bet this interview with you was about the longest one he gave in maybe the last ten years of his life," Hinton told *SI* later. "He just wasn't doing them. It was all part of creating this broader image they thought was necessary."

I was the replacement for Hinton. A senior writer at *SI,* I was a general assigment reporter, covering all sports, not a NASCAR expert. I did write a story a year for the NASCAR issue—a year earlier I had been in Dawsonville, Georgia, talking to former moonshiners and revenue agents and to Bill Elliott's father about the roots of the sport—but mostly I was a casual follower of Winston Cup proceedings. I knew Earnhardt only by reputation, by the pack of newspaper clippings the magazine sent me. The Intimidator, huh? This was interesting.

"I have only one piece of advice," Earnhardt's publicity man and handler, J. R. Rhodes, said on the phone. "Don't mention Hinton's name. You do that and the interview's over. That's the way Dale is."

I said I understood. J. R., too, said Earnhardt didn't do many interviews. He said *ESPN,* the magazine, also was angling to do a story. Earnhardt had refused.

"Why's that?" I asked.

"We don't like that writer either," Rhodes said.

———————

The plan was to drive with Earnhardt from Ann Arbor, Michigan, to Brooklyn, Michigan. Earnhardt was doing a noontime autograph session and speech to several hundred Goodwrench dealers in a large ballroom at the Crowne Plaza. A car would be waiting, engine running, at the conclusion of his talk and J. R. would be at a side door and WE'LL BE GETTING OUT OF THERE RIGHT AWAY, BE ON TIME. Elvis would leave the building, no nonsense, and be headed for the Michigan International Speedway, the site of the weekend's Pepsi 400. The trip would take perhaps an hour, an hour and a half. That was interview time. J. R. would drive me back to the hotel.

On the prescribed day, the schedule was pushed up at the last minute. J. R. never called with this information, so I arrived at the ball-room, thinking I was early, but Earnhardt already was finishing the speech to the Goodwrench dealers, opening the floor to questions. The autograph session was done. I slid into a table near the door where J. R. stood.

My first impression was how quiet the room was, how attentive the dealers were, how . . . adoring. They listened with a polite inten-stity, as if they were hearing General Norman Schwarzkopf detail the Persian Gulf War or the Reverend Billy Graham chart out the AAA-approved route to Heaven. Earnhardt was good at this. The years of polishing had turned out a public-relations entertainer when he wanted to be. Executives of large companies, graduates of famous schools, often are tongue-tied and dull when forced to stand in front of the stockholders and give an annual report. This was a man who knew how to speak.

He told little anecdotes, making fun of himself. He talked about his team's progress during the season. He introduced crew members in the audience. Everything was light and easy. He defended his use of the open helmet. ("They haven't ruled it out," he said. "So I still wear it. I don't want my son to wear it, but I wear it.") He described his collision with his son in an IROC race a year earlier in June at Michigan.

The story was classic. Driving similarly prepared Pontiacs, father and son came to the last lap running first and second. This was the sec-ond time they ever had raced each other, the first time they were close during the end of a race. Son tried to pass father on the high side. There was a collision. Son went spinning. Father won the race. There was a dispute about who hit whom.

"I show him the pictures," Earnhardt said. "He ran into me. I said, 'If I ran into you, how'd we get back down here on the track?' I show him the angle. Is there any doubt?"

He finished the explanation with a look that professional wrestlers make when they are checked for use of a foreign substance in the ring. Who, me? Yeah, there was doubt.

The dealers had a string of knowledgeable questions. Earnhardt had thoughtful answers. He said ten, fifteen years ago he didn't handle these functions as well. He knew the routine now and was at ease. He had talked to the same kind of group a week earlier in Indianapolis before he raced in the Brickyard 400.

One of the last questions concerned his car, the Monte Carlo. A replica of the car had been placed on the grass outside the hotel.

"Everying I have," Earnhardt said in response, "is because of that black No. 3 car out there."

———————

Earnhardt sat in the shotgun seat, seat belt fastened. Rhodes, the publicity man, drove. I sat in the backseat. The rented Chevrolet, another Monte Carlo, without the decals, was gone, whipping out of the parking lot before one Goodwrench dealer put a spoon into one fruit cup.

"Now, the turn is up here, J. R.," Earnhardt said.

"I know," Rhodes replied.

"And watch that truck over there."

"I know."

The route was along U.S. Highway 12, the old road to Chicago from Detroit before I-94 was built. Neglected by developers for forty or fifty years, the action moved to the north, the road now was a preserved stretch of America, circa post–Korean War. It soon rolled past farmlands and through small towns. A string of Bates Motels, boasting color TV (!), gave way to miniature golf courses and antique shops and flea markets and roadside taverns that looked as if they could become nasty on a Saturday night.

Earnhardt knew the road after years of going to the speedway and pointed out interesting auto salvage yards and potential hunting sites and a bar where fans often gathered before the races. He said he'd wave to them when he saw them, back when drivers stayed at hotels instead of the modern motor coaches in the infield. There were a number of ads at taverns and stores with his picture on the front and other ads with his son's picture. He never mentioned any of them. Someone had painted "I HATE JEFF GORDON" on a rock. He also didn't mention that.

A one-sided dialogue throughout the trip was more advice for Rhodes at the wheel. Earnhardt was a constant backseat driver. ("A control freak," one longtime NASCAR writer later explained. "Of course he is. There isn't a driver out there who isn't a control freak.") Rhodes seemed used to the routine.

"Watch it. That light's going to change."

"I know."

"And you'd better get in the right lane."

The interview went surprisingly well. Earnhardt had shaved his mustache the week before the Brickyard. On a trip to the Caribbean with Teresa and Taylor, he found that he had trouble snorkeling because the mask wouldn't seal against the hair on his upper lip. He simply shaved off the hair. This turned out to be huge news when he reached Indy. He was supposed to shoot a commercial for Coca-Cola and the producers wanted him to wear a fake mustache and he refused. The shoot was postponed. He now had a shoot with Upper Deck bubblegum cards scheduled. The mustache was only back to stubble. He didn't know what these people would say, but again he wasn't going to wear a false mustache.

"It's amazing, this thing with the mustache," he said. "It's, like, big news. In *Entertainment Weekly,* I think it is, they list the ten happenings of the week. One of them this week was 'Earnhardt shaves off his mustache.' Here we are, NASCAR goes to Indy. Dale Jarrett wins the race. That's never mentioned. It's all about Earnhardt's mustache. Silly."

I also had a mustache, also had found snorkeling was tough. He mentioned the fact. A door was opened to some mustache talk. I said I'd grown mine on my thirtieth birthday, something to do to mark the occasion. Earnhardt said he'd had his since 1982, just about the same age. Maybe there was some rite-of-passage business here. Something.

The conversation went from there. There are interviews that are strict business arrangements, resembling the televised-press-conference sort of stuff that you see reprinted by the Merkle Press or someone, and there are interviews that are rambles, give-and-take, natural. This was a ramble.

Earnhardt talked about his son the way your neighbor would talk about his son. The kid was wonderful, love him dearly, but the things he does! The kid doesn't get up in the morning, wastes half his day in bed! The kid doesn't focus! The kid has to learn!

Earnhardt said he, himself, was up at four most mornings, always in the shower by 5:30. He had the house to himself! He could get things done. Teresa and Taylor would be up at seven, Taylor getting ready for school. He would be moving already! The kid, Dale Jr., doesn't even think about getting up until 8:30! Doesn't he know what he's missing? Snort. The kid is up half the night on that computer! Life isn't lived on the computer! Life is lived in the living!

In conversational, synopsis fashion, Earnhardt detailed his life story. Growing up with Ralph, his own race-driver father. Idolizing Ralph. The joy in the house when Ralph won a race, aunts and uncles and friends gathering in the house in Kannapolis for a country ham breakfast at midnight, the party lasting until dawn. The story about the one race he ran against Ralph, his father pushing him past the disgruntled other driver into third place. The two hasty early marriages. The third with Teresa that stuck. The arrival of Kelley and Dale Jr. after the fire at their mother's house. The arrival of Kerry after his sixteenth birthday. The constant round of traveling that kept him pretty much out of his kids' lives until now. ("Teresa raised 'em. I didn't do much, I have to admit.") The joy at seeing everyone grown and OK. The joy at having a second chance with Taylor, now eight.

"She's with us wherever we go," he said. "She knows more adults than she does children. She's driving already. I've got her driving a big pickup truck around the farm. She has her own golf cart. She rides horses."

Dale Jr.'s success clearly pleased Earnhardt. He said he felt closer now to his son than ever. They were exploring each other, becoming friends, really, finding out things they never knew. The Busch series race usually was held the day before the Winston race at the same track. Father and son would talk in each other's motor homes on Thursday or Friday, talk about anything and everything, about the difficulties of turn four at Daytona or the struggles of the Atlanta Braves or the plans for Christmas dinner.

Earnhardt had his first true driving buddy and confidant at the track since Neil Bonnett died. He didn't say this, but it was true.

"I never thought Dale Jr. was going to be a race driver," Earnhardt said. "He never seemed to have the interest. He wasn't one of those kids who always wanted to be around the garage, to see how things worked. What's happened has kind of surprised me."

When Kerry joined the family—Dale Jr., thirteen at the time, and Kelley, fifteen, never even had met him—there was an increase in interest in the father's sport. Kerry and Dale Jr. began fooling around with cars, engines. They worked on an old '78 Monte Carlo, getting it ready for racing. When Earnhardt saw the situation, he stepped in and added a roll bar, a harness, "all the safety stuff," and just let the kids keep working. This was their deal.

For a season, the two reunited half brothers raced the car on local short tracks. They alternated weeks as drivers, figuring out the sport for themselves. Earnhardt, pleased, offered to prepare two identical race cars for the next season so each son could drive. Kelley raised her hand. Couldn't a girl drive, too? What's the story? Earnhardt said he would prepare three race cars.

Off they went, the racing Earnhardts. They usually didn't compete against each other, separate races at separate tracks, but they came home and compared notes. Who finished higher? Who crashed? The best finisher said he or she was the best driver. The worst finisher blamed the car. Family stuff.

"Kelley was very good," Earnhardt said. "If she stayed with it . . . I liked the way she drove. It just got hard for her. There's a thing in racing, like it or not, that men don't like preparing a car for a woman. She had an awful time finding guys to work on her car. Finally, that got to her. She took a job and quit. I still think she could be a good driver. Maybe she'll come back someday. She wants to drive bad.

"Kerry just crashes too much. He's still driving and it might work out, but he's married now, a couple of kids, and can't give the sport the attention it needs. It's hard when you have kids. He's still driving. I try to help him, but I don't know.

"Dale Jr., he's been the surprise."

It turned out that maybe the kid never wanted to clean the wrenches, sweep the floor, follow the path that his father had followed in that little garage in Kannapolis—different times, different situations—but, once started, he wanted to know more and more about cars. In five years, he had made spectacular progress. Busch champion. Starting in Winston Cup. Face in the Budweiser ads. There were people who said already he would be a better driver than his father. Smoother. More like Ralph, saving equipment, making the rush at the end. Not as impetuous.

The father was proud.

"It's great to share all this with your son," he said. "He's doing the same things you do. He has the same problems. He's meeting with sponsors, signing autographs, doing the stuff that maybe had begun to tire you out. It's all new to him. It's exciting. He brings back the excitement. It makes me want to keep doing this."

As the rented Monte Carlo reached the track, Earnhardt began giving more directions. ("You know where the turn is, J. R., right?") He talked about his finishes at Michigan, where he'd won twice. He pointed out the helicopter pad, where a chopper was leaving at that moment. He said he would be at the helicopter pad ten minutes after the race unless he won. He would be at a private airport ten minutes after that, on the Learjet, heading home.

"I'll be in North Carolina before you're back to your hotel," he told the writer. "It's the way you have to do it. Or you don't have any free time."

On impulse, he told J. R. to pull out the cell phone. Call Junior! See how he did in qualifying for the Busch! J. R. called. He said Junior had qualified third. Junior thought everything went well.

"Is he there?" Earnhardt said. "Tell him I want to see him. I'll be there in five minutes."

"He's going out," J. R. said. "He's leaving right now. He's going to the mall."

"Going to the mall! Tell him to get me a present. Tell him to buy his father something. Tell him to buy me . . . tell him to buy me a CD. . . . Tell him to buy me the new Alison Krauss CD!"

"Who?"

"Alison Krauss!"

A look of satisfaction came across the father's famous face. Yes! His son would buy him a CD. A present. Alison Krauss. The interview was done.

I decided I liked Earnhardt, at least the version I had met. The man seemed to have a sense of fulfillment in middle age, a completeness (is that a word?) to his life. He was well into middle age, forty-seven. The biggest battles already had been fought. The mistakes of youth had been made, the indiscretions and the misdirections all had been committed or followed. The page on all that had been turned. He was watching his youngest daughter, Taylor, grow and develop, finding a wonder at home that he had been too busy to see with his other kids when he was just charging, charging to the front. He was where he wanted to be. There was no doubt about that. No one could take away what he already had accomplished, the seven championships, the empire, no matter what. This extra time at the top was a blessing. Nothing less.

I was used to dealing with twenty-year-olds, kids who were around Dale Jr.'s age. These are the red blood cells of sport, the fuel that makes the engine work. They usually are muscle machines, stronger or faster or more coordinated than the average human being. They have a gift that makes them a half second faster in the 40-yard dash, a head taller when they jump, eyesight that can pick up the spin of a baseball. Money falls from the sky around them. They almost can't help but be self-centered and vain, living in this one dimension that has brought them fame, glory, and a fine collection of body art.

Earnhardt was old enough to have perspective.

"I've done things in business that would have made my father go crazy," he said once in the interview. "He was a guy who paid cash for everything he ever owned. A house. A car. He saved and bought them. I remember once he went for a loan for something. The only time he went that I know. He didn't get the loan. The banker said, 'Where's your credit history?' My father didn't have one. He'd never had a loan. The banker said, 'Well, we can't give you the money if you have no credit history.' My father said he'd paid for everything he ever bought. Never needed a loan. The banker said, 'Sorry.'

"My father's thing was 'Never buy anything on credit that you can't look at while you're paying for it,'" I said in response. "That's kind of the same thing. 'Don't buy a vacation or a night on the town on Saturday and have to pay for it on Monday. Buy a refrigerator, OK, because you'll still be using that refrigerator while you write out the checks. You can see what you're getting.'"

Earnhardt shook his head. Yes.

He most resembled . . . who? I thought about it. My eventual answer was Nolan Ryan. I had gone to Alvin, Texas, and done a long story on the Hall of Fame baseball pitcher in the last year of his career. Ryan very much resembled Earnhardt. He was forty-six years old at the time, still competitive, still good. Excellence had brought him to a certain place, rich and famous, businesses everywhere, but longevity had brought him to another. He knew exactly how good his life was. He knew exactly what mattered. He also didn't have a grand formal education, but he had learned the right lessons by necessity, by trial and error, everything in public. He also had a strong wife who had kept the package together, both at home and in business. He also was still a master at what he did, still challenged hitters every night, but he had a base level of satisfaction. This was all extra, a dessert of the good life.

"Nolan Ryan and Dale Earnhardt," I decided. "They both still have their fastballs."

———————

The interview with Dale Jr. took place the next day. There were problems getting it arranged. The old NASCAR, before the media was called "the media," was an easygoing operation. The older writers talk about wandering from garage to garage at the speedways, walking through the door and saying, "Hey, Richard, how's that car running?" or "Benny, why'd you go into a slide in Turn Two, hit the wall, and then roll over a half dozen times?" This does not happen now. Every move is tied to rights fees, to endorsement exposure, to a quid pro quo of "What will you do for me if I do this for you?" Money rules. The drivers are in trailers, isolated. A phalanx of PR people from the various sponsors stand in front doing close-order drills with their cell phones, the spit-shined Palace Guard keeping Queen Elizabeth away from the masses.

There was a collection of PR people at work here. Each of them made easy promises. This will be done! Each of them disappeared. Nothing happened.

Luckily, Dale Jr. won the Busch race on Saturday. He beat out Jeff Gordon for his third win of the season. After driving his Winston Cup car for happy hour, a final practice run for the next day's race, Junior then did a winner's press conference. The Bud PR man was in attendance. The Bud PR man said he would make things happen.

At the end of the press conference, he approached Junior. Junior was holding the trophy and flowers for his Busch win. The PR man tried to set up the time for an interview. Junior thumbed through the PalmPilot of his mind and said, "Let's do it now." Now? He sat back down at the press conference table. Now? I took a seat next to him. There were maybe thirty people still in the room, hanging around. They sat back down. They listened to the questions, laughed or nodded at the answers. The interview resembled the *Oprah Winfrey Show.* This was a Merkle Press job.

Junior, nevertheless, was candid.

He talked about growing up with—or maybe without—a famous absentee father. The story about his father's youth, sitting around the kitchen table all night, eating breakfast after Ralph came home with the trophy and a couple of hundred bucks to pay the bills? Junior said he'd never even heard that story, but it sounded great. He said that was something he always wanted, something that never happened. His own dad would leave straight from the track to a hunting trip. Or an appearance. Something.

The part about not wanting to be a driver when he was a kid? He *always* wanted to be a driver. He just didn't want to sweep the garage floor. The part about school? His dad always talked the importance of going to school. He was hung up on the fact that he had quit school after ninth grade. There were fights about school. Dale Jr. didn't like school. His father sent him for two years to military school. The place was so grim, his sister, Kelley, signed up for the same school, just to help him through the experience. OK, maybe it helped, especially with personal habits. He learned how to brush his teeth the right way. Overall, though, school?

"It was such a big thing to my father, but where was he the night I graduated?" Junior said. "He was someplace else on the other side of the earth. Why wasn't he there? I understand, I guess, but I wanted to hold that diploma right in his face, to show him that I'd done it. And he just wasn't there."

Only now was a true relationship being established. That was Junior's thought. There were childhood stories to tell—the time his father almost killed him, trying to pull him on water skis, the time his father took him for driving lessons at the go-kart track, the time his father cut himself with a chain saw and kept on sawing until the tree was down, blood be damned—but the last two years were the first time for talks. This was the first burst of equality, man-to-man stuff. This was all new.

And the time his father and he collided at Michigan in the IROC race? Whose fault was that?

"Are you kidding?" Junior said. "He slammed me. No doubt about it."

I decided I liked Junior, too. Junior had spirit.

In the following months, I followed the adventures of the two Earnhardts. That happens. If you meet people, work with them, like them well enough, you tend to follow what they do. God forbid, counter to all the journalism school rules, you root for them.

The race the very next week in Bristol, after both Earnhardts finished out of the money in Michigan, was a fine example of the possibilities for fun. The father caught Terry Labonte on the backstretch of the last lap in the bandbox track and cruised home with the win. Well, he did more than catch Labonte. He caught Labonte, gave him a tidy little bump, sent Labonte spinning, and flew past for the trophy. Poor Labonte finished eighth.

"Terry caught me coming to the white flag in turns three and four," Earnhardt explained. "When we went back to turn one, I went back up there to get with him and get under him. Whether he checked up or I got in deeper or what. I bumped him too hard and turned him loose. It spun him. I didn't mean to do it intentionally. I meant to get in there and race with him, but I know he's not going to see it that way. I know he's upset. He has a right to be."

"I know he hit me intentionally," Labonte said. "If he hadn't, he wouldn't have hit me in the center of my back bumper. Now, if he had tried to pass me and had gotten into me, that would have been a different deal."

Was this better than the other offerings inside the cable clicker or what? Labonte fumed. Earnhardt smiled and collected the winner's check like some Oil Can Harry villain. *Yeeeeeow.* This could be a lot of fun.

I paid attention. I began to notice the number of cars and trucks on the road with the No. 3 and/or No. 8 pasted on the bumper or back window. (With the Chevy trucks there usually also was a decal on the window of some wild-eyed little baby pissing on a Ford logo.) I began to watch the races on television more often than not. I hooked into the trick of watching that No. 3 car on the move, no matter where it was on the track. I was not disappointed.

For the rest of the season and through the 2000 schedule, I watched Earnhardts. The old man was indeed revitalized. The 2000 season was a wonder. He finished second in the Winston Cup standings by only 265 votes to champion Bobby Labonte. He won twice, was second five times, had a string of eight straight top tens in the middle of the season, and finished every race. He very definitely was back in the hunt. The Talladega race was as good as any race he had ever driven. Junior was an instant sensation. He won twice and added the Winston, the all-star race in the middle of the season at Lowe's Speedway, to the total. His father joined him in the victory circle, father and son, all-stars, at the top of the world, yet no more than thirty miles from where it all began.

Were they getting closer? I wondered.

In the middle of the 2000 season, Junior wrote a tribute to his father, read it to him, choked him up, in fact, and posted it on the NASCAR Web site.

"His friendship is the greatest gift you could ever obtain," Dale Jr. wrote in part. "Out of all his attributes, it is the most impressive. He trusts only a few with this gift. If you ever break that trust—it is over. He accepts few apologies. Many have crossed him and they leave only with regret for their actions. In every result, he stands as an example of what hard work and dedication will achieve. Even his enemies know this.

"I have had the pleasure of joining him on the battlefield. I have experienced his intimidating wrath. This may sound strong, but I know what I am talking about. He roams like a lion, king of his jungle. His jungle is his and his alone. Every step he takes has purpose. Every walk has reason.

"He praises God, loves his family, enjoys his friends. . . ."

How much closer?

Junior had become known as a man to be noticed around the Charlotte nightclub scene. He had moved out of the double-wide on the Earnhardt property and moved into his own house across the road from the DEI headquarters in Mooresville. He had built his own club, The Club E, complete with ear-blowing stereo speakers, a head-bending giant television screen, a cooler large enough to fit thirteen cases of beer, black leather bar stools, mirrored walls, and purple neon. There also were women involved. Junior had dates.

What did Dad think about all of this? Dad somehow seemed to know all about the dates. The man who didn't know his kids very well for most of their lives now seemed to know everything about them.

"It's really weird, man," Junior told *SI*. "He'll ask me about how the date went and he'll know more about her than me. I guess he's trying to make sure I don't make any bad decisions."

Dad and Junior seemed fine.

In August of 2000, I had another tough NASCAR assignment. The ugly and feared side of the sport had reemerged. Adam Petty and Kenny Irwin had died in practice crashes in New Hampshire. Young Tony Roper had died in a crash in the Craftsman truck series. Three deaths, all apparently by the same cause, a basal skull fracture, gave NASCAR its worst string of deaths in recent years.

I was sent to Level Cross, North Carolina, to talk with Kyle Petty about the death of his son, slightly over two months after the crash. What do you say to a father in this situation? What do you ask? This was the most famous family in the sport. Adam Petty was nineteen years old. I had kids around that age. The thought of losing either of them took my breath away. Where do you even start?

"Some days I think I'm doing OK," Kyle Petty said, trying to explain. "Then, other days, I say, 'I'm not OK at all. . . . I'm back at the beginning.'"

He was a lovely man, Kyle Petty. Sitting in the large office of his own father, the fabled Richard, in the family compound of offices and a museum and a couple of houses, he unrolled his emotions in an even, fond voice. He said he didn't mind talking about Adam. He enjoyed it. The more he talked about Adam, the more Adam was on his mind. He liked having Adam on his mind.

"I loved him so much," Kyle said. "He gave me a whole new look at this business, seeing it through his eyes. If you've been around it for a while—the sponsors, the appearances, the meetings—it can become stale. You become jaded. He saw things that I couldn't see anymore."

He talked—as Earnhardt talked—about the beauty of being in the same business with your son. He talked about the time spent at the track, the Thursdays and Fridays. He talked about the closeness that had developed, father and son, so much closeness that he worried that he was neglecting his other two kids, which was why he had taken his daughter, Montgomery Lee, to England on the weekend that Adam died. He talked about the loss, the pain, now that all that close contact was done.

"The moment I got that phone call, my childhood was over," Petty said. "Though I was forty years old, until then I had been an eighteen-year-old kid inside, driving a race car, enjoying myself. I didn't worry about anything. Now the kid is gone."

The deaths of Adam and the other drivers had brought back the realities of driving race cars. Putting yourself in that car was putting your mortality at risk. Simple as that. This was a loud, flamboyant, exciting game, but it also was just about the most deadly game ever invented.

I thought about the Pettys and also thought about the Earnhardts. How do you do this? How do you let your kids do this? I worried for Dale Jr.

For some reason, I never worried about the father. Not once.

10

The checks and cards and letters and packages started arriving almost as soon as Teresa Earnhardt spoke. The Foundation for the Carolinas was overwhelmed.

"We wound up hiring six part-time people to come in," Charity Perkins, vice president for public relations, says. "We needed them every day for a month."

Teresa gave the organization's address on the Monday after the accident. The Earnhardts had established the Earnhardt Fund in 1997 anonymously. The foundation collects gifts and then distributes them to the charities selected by the Earnhardts.

The gifts now arrived by the hundreds, by the thousands. By that Monday afternoon, the flood tide had begun. More than 10,000 gifts would be received in the next month.

"The number three played a role in a lot of the gifts," Perkins says. "We'd receive checks for $33 or $333, something like that. The ones that touched you the most were from little children. The children would enclose a poem or a drawing of a car and then 33 cents would fall out.

"A lot of people have asked if everything came from the South. That wasn't the case at all. There were gifts from everywhere around the United States, from foreign countries. There was all kinds of memorabilia that people sent that will be auctioned off."

The address for the Foundation for the Carolinas is P.O. Box 34769, Charlotte, N.C., 28234-4769. Perkins says the Foundation cannot release a dollar figure on how much has been received. The six part-time workers have been released, but donations have arrived at an uneven pace in succeeding months, triggered by nostalgic events on the NASCAR circuit.

A large bump occurred around April 29, 2001. Dale Earnhardt's fiftieth birthday . . .

DAYTONA 2001

The *Orlando Sentinel* ran a three-part series in the middle of the 2001 Daytona Speed Week that now, later, reads like an eerie blueprint of the immediate future. The series was about NASCAR safety and auto-racing death. The timing was pretty much an accident.

"The deaths of Adam Petty and Kenny Irwin and Tony Roper in the summer of 2000 caught our attention," *Sentinel* sports editor Van McKenzie says. "There was an obvious pattern, all three drivers dying from the same injury, a basal skull fracture. We started on the series right after Kenny Irwin died in New Hampshire in July. The idea was to get it out as soon as we could."

"It wasn't an easy series to do," Ed Hinton, the lead writer on the project, says. "It took time, because you were dealing with Formula One, Indy, all the different kinds of racing. By the time everything was put together and done, we were into the middle of November. Football was going strong and the NBA and hockey were starting up, and if you ran the thing then, it would have been lost. So we decided to hold it for the week of the Daytona 500 in February."

The first article was an historical look at auto-racing deaths. The words were harrowing. Mario Andretti, the Indy legend, described how he still has nightmares about dying in a crash. Emerson Fittipaldi, the onetime Formula One champion, remembered sitting at the drivers' meeting at Monte Carlo, looking at the twenty-two men in the room, and realizing three of them would not be alive at the end of the season. Which three? That was how bad the odds were at the time.

The simple recitation of death after death was a reminder of how grim the sport can be. The happy television ads for Fox and NBC or UPS or McDonald's or an assortment of beers always seem to forget that fact. The weekly stories, the results, forget it. Everybody around NASCAR—look no further than the historical chronicle in the press guide that doesn't mention deaths—conveniently forgets it.

No other game in our modern culture has scarier statistics concerning fatality rates than auto racing. Not bullfighting. Not boxing. Not hang gliding. The *Sentinel*'s list of fallen heroes, starting with the Marquis de Montaignac at Course de Perigueux in France in 1898 and running straight to Petty and Irwin in New Hampshire in 2000, was startling. Hundreds of men have died driving race cars.

The most famous death occurred on May 1, 1994. The best race car driver in the world, Formula One champion Ayrton Senna, died when his Williams FW16 racer shot off the course at the San Marino Grand Prix and hit a concrete retaining wall at 180 miles per hour. The thirty-two-year-old Brazilian was killed instantly, not only from a piece of shrapnel that pierced his helmet, but also from basal skull fracture, the violent whipping motion of his head and neck under high G-forces at impact.

For many of the crashes, many of the deaths, rationalization came easily as the show tooted along to the next noisy stop. The driver was too young, too inexperienced . . . a piece of equipment failed . . . there was something wrong with the tires . . . there could be none of that with Senna. If the best driver in the world could die in a crash, no one on a racetrack was immune.

In the final part of the series, titled "Nascar Idles While Drivers Die," safety issues were addressed. NASCAR was cited as the slowest mover among racing bodies in the march toward racing safety. The lack of a full-time, traveling medical staff was noted. The resistance to change—especially in encouraging the use of the HANS (head and neck support system)—was noted. The lack of significant safety testing was noted.

One of the possible safety additions mentioned was the so-called soft walls. Did the walls of a track have to be hard concrete, built to protect the fans but do nothing for the drivers? Wouldn't some impact-absorbing material be much safer? One of the knocks against the idea was that too much time would be needed to clean off the track after a driver hit the wall and the wall shattered more than the car did. One of the voices speaking in favor of the soft walls was Dale Earnhardt.

"I'd rather they spend twenty minutes cleaning up that mess," he said, "than cleaning me off the wall."

———————

If any of the facts in the series bothered him—indeed, if he'd even seen the articles—Earnhardt gave no indication. Life was good at Speed Week. Life was wonderful. He was elder statesman and title contender all in one. Respected, yet still vital. His DEI team had expanded to three cars—Michael Waltrip joining Dale Jr. and Steve Park—and his own No. 3 car for RCR certainly was competitive. The possible eighth championship, once seen almost as a certainty, then as out of the question, now seemed within his grasp. Richard Petty, watch out.

The Intimidator was back.

"I had a great talk with him last October," Larry McReynolds, whose two-year stint with Earnhardt ended badly, says. "Our daughters go to the same school, the same class. They went on a field trip for the day to the space center in Huntsville, Alabama, and when I went to pick up my daughter that night, Dale was there, too, waiting. The bus was thirty minutes late and it was raining. I got into Dale's Tahoe and we just talked.

"The conversation drifted to different areas, but wound up in the time I'd spent with him. He said, 'You know, I just hate that you came along at such a bad time.' He said he'd had neck surgery before the 2000 season, clearing up problems from the crash in Talladega in '96, and it had made all the difference in the world. He said he never realized how bad he'd felt until he had the surgery. I don't think any of us, even him, realized how hurt he was."

McReynolds thought back to the two years. Earnhardt's constant complaint through those down times was "I just don't feel comfortable in the car." He said it a million times. Well, of course he didn't feel comfortable. He was hurt. Since the surgery, think about it, he was right back in the hunt in 2000, winning races, finishing second in the points race. He was as good as he had ever been.

"He had that surgery," McReynolds says, "and he came right out of the box. He was on the mend. I was thinking that he was going to have a great year."

Earnhardt's enthusiasm for the new year was obvious. The rise of Dale Jr. was still a wonder to behold. They were partners as much as father and son, partners and competitors and boss and employee, a great and lovely family-bonding package. The joy of it all had been seen in the first weekend of the month right here at Daytona. For the first time in his life, Dale Earnhardt had gone road racing a month earlier, driving with Junior and veteran sports car racers Andy Pilgrim and Kelly Collins in the 24 Hours of Daytona.

Started in 1962 as a three-hour road race, the 24 Hours of Daytona has become the American answer to the 24 Hours of LeMans, a test of a car's durabiliy more than a driver's prowess. Four-man driving teams share the wheel on the course set up inside the Speedway. The cars are different and the event is different from the more-publicized action of Speed Week, two weeks later. The drivers also are usually different.

Usually.

"Christmas and New Year's were over," Earnhardt said. "I'd always been interested in the race and I was getting a little bored."

What was it Pilgrim said?

"You've been taking the bypass around the track," he told Earnhardt. "Now you have to take the business route."

This was entirely new, this business of sharing and driving the twists and turns of the 3.56-mile road puzzle through rain and darkness and whatever conditions might arise. Earnhardt always had resisted the lure of other forms of racing, unlike, say, Andretti and A. J. Foyt, Indy heroes who came to NASCAR and Formula One and road racing, tackling any form of driving that was out there. Earnhardt was a specialist. He was dirt tracks, asphalt, stock cars. He always had a roof over his head. He specialized at turning left at high speeds. NASCAR guys mostly stayed NASCAR guys.

"The best description of NASCAR I ever heard came from an Englishman, no less," Humpy Wheeler says. "Alan Jones came to Charlotte one year to drive in a Can-Am race. He somehow struck up a friendship with Richard Petty. They just got along. Petty let him drive his car a couple of times and then Jones, after his race, stayed around to watch the Charlotte 600.

"I came up to him in the press box and offered him a chance to come back the next year and drive in the race. For years, drivers in other series always put down NASCAR, called it 'taxicab racing.' Jones wasn't like that. He'd driven the car. He started stammering. 'Well, I couldn't, no, really . . . I mean I could, but it would take a year of practice. No.' He said, in the end, 'This isn't auto racing, it's a bloody black art.' I always loved that, 'bloody black art.'"

Wheeler told the aging modern master of the bloody black art that he would have to sleep on a cot during the 24 Hours of Daytona. That was an historical lie. Drivers used to sleep on cots, but no longer do. Earnhardt bit at the lie.

"I'm not sleeping on any damn cot," he said.

"Well, those are the rules," Wheeler said.

"Well, the rules are changing," Earnhardt said. "I'm sleeping in a bed in the motor coach."

The race was a sweet experience. The father and the son figured out the new problems on the different course in the different cars, Corvettes, in this different around-the-clock event. They finished fourth, second in their GTS division, even getting to sample some lightning and rain. Another Corvette team won the race, so father and son joined the victory celebration, squirting champagne on the fans. The fans loved it. The Earnhardts were the highlight of the race.

Pilgrim had an interesting observation on the approaches of the father and son as drivers.

"Dale Jr. was completely fearless," the road race veteran said. "He was not intimidated by the car. He kinda came from the top and realized you can't drive the car completely 100 percent all the time. He's come down to a point where he now understands running pace.

"Dale came the other way. He wasn't using his brakes hard and was more respectful of the car. He's come up from that and they are both running very similar times and seem to be pretty comfortable and understand what you need to do in a twenty-four-hour race."

Respectful of the car? Starting slow and building up? The father sounded as if he had become his own father, Ralph. The son . . . well, the son was the same as Ralph's son had been, too. Life was good. Life was wonderful.

———

In 1998, Earnhardt had written his autobiography. Sort of. He approached veteran sportswriter Benny Phillips from the *High Point Enterprise* at a racetrack and said, "Hey, somebody's finally come up with enough money for me to do a book and you're writing it." The deal was set. All Benny had to do was find him.

"Trying to run him down was like trying to run down Franklin Delano Roosevelt," Phillips says. "It was always 'We'll do it, we'll do it' . . . and then he was gone. I finally got fed up. He had no idea about the amount of time that was involved. He thought it was like an interview for a newspaper story. The publisher was pushing me and I had nothing. I just called him up, in the end, and said, 'I'm not doing your book. I'm done with it.' Of course, we sat down the next day and he was great. He got into it 200 percent. It was like everything in his life. It was a challenge. He'd say, 'I hear Jeff Gordon's doing a book. Our book's going to be better.' "

Phillips would drive to Earnhardt's farm in Mooresville. He'd find his man signing autographs, talking on the phone, making deals, answering a billion questions, making a billion decisions. The two men would go to the only refuge available, Earnhardt's truck. They would drive around his 900 acres and eventually stop at some scenic spot and Phillips would take out his tape recorder and Earnhardt would talk.

Phillips was an old aquaintance, if not total friend. He had the feeling that Earnhardt had few total friends. Neil Bonnett certainly had been a total friend, but the rest of the people . . . Phillips had the feeling that more people considered themselves Earnhardt's friend than Earnhardt considered as his friends. Did that make sense?

"I mean, like, Rusty Wallace was supposed to be a friend," Phillips says. "Darrell Waltrip. I'm sure they considered themselves friends, but if you saw them with Dale, you always saw them with him at his trailer. You never saw him with them at their trailers. You know what I mean? He was a private person."

Phillips had hunted and fished with Earnhardt for a number of years. He remembers hunting with Earnhardt and Terry Labonte at the close of 1979, the Rookie of the Year season. Earnhardt was talking forever about how thrilled he was to earn almost $30,000 for the year. Think of that. Think of where he came from to where he eventually landed. Think.

"The thing that most surprised me about him, doing the book, was how religious he was," Phillips says. "I had never known that. Most of our talk was straight-ahead stuff, barbershop talk, nothing about religion or politics, but he did say that he prayed a lot. He said he didn't pray to win a race, because he didn't think God cared about that, but he did pray that nobody got hurt. He talked about going to church as a kid. He was a religious man."

The religious side, which had grown and grown in later years, had been shown mostly through deed more than words. There are a number of outspoken Christians on the NASCAR circuit—Waltrip and Jeff Gordon at the top of the list—but Earnhardt's faith was more quiet. He was a voice on the phone to a terminally ill patient, a visitor to a hospital room, a silent benefactor to farmers in need. His charity was quiet charity.

"He was Lutheran, which is a more quiet denomination," Father Dale Grubda, a Catholic priest and racing photographer from Wisconsin, a friend, says. "His religion was more . . . northern, if that's the word. He wasn't like the Baptists, so outspoken."

In the nineties, Earnhardt did become active in Motor Racing Outreach, a ministry directed by Reverend Max Helton. Helton arrived on the scene in 1988, running Sunday-morning services for the drivers and crews. He found himself preaching to a hard-living congregation. He would look from the pulpit and see maybe three drivers in the crowd.

"Now it's completely changed," he says. "I'd say 75 percent of the drivers are at the service. Dale was one of them. I found him to be very thoughtful of other people. Very kind and generous. Around '93 or '94, a couple of drivers asked me to pray with them before races. I agreed, but got to thinking that I really shouldn't be showing favoritism to anyone. So I announced that I was available for any driver to pray before a race. Dale was the first to say, 'Yeah, I'd like that.' It kind of surprised me at the time, because I didn't know him that well and there was all of the Intimidator reputation . . . but privately he was much different."

"Yes, I believe in the Bible and the Lord, and I pray a lot, more than I ever prayed in my life," Earnhardt said in his book with Phillips. "But I never have asked the Lord to let me win a race. The way I figure it, there are a lot of people in this world and I don't believe God has time for trivial things. I doubt He would consider it important, someone asking for help driving a race car. . . ."

The book, titled *Dale Earnhardt, Determined,* did not dwell on religion. It was a different sort of autobiography, probably not an autobiography at all, a coffee table book filled with lush racing pictures and chunks of italic quotes from Earnhardt and other text by Phillips and coauthor Ben Blake. Phillips remembers that the passionate parts of the interviews were about Earnhardt's father, his family, and, certainly, most of all, racing.

"Cup your left hand," Phillips says. "Now take your right hand and slam it into the cup of your left hand like an ax. Do it again and again. That was how Earnhardt talked one day when we talked about racing.

"He said, 'Lots of people like to eat. *(Slam.)* Lots of people like to do other things. *(Slam.)* I like to race! *(Slam.)* There's nothing like it. *(Slam.)* Being next to the other guy. *(Slam.)* Side by side. *(Slam.)* Door to door. *(Slam.)* Right in there, rooting *(Slam)*, pawing *(Slam)*, digging *(Slam)*, into the turns."

Slam. That was still the spirit inside the forty-nine-year-old man at Daytona.

Kirk Shelmerdine came around during Speed Week to visit the man he'd helped win four Winston Cup titles. They hadn't seen each other for a while and went to Earnhardt's motor home. Shelmerdine had forgotten how busy royalty can be.

"It was Tuesday, maybe Wednesday," Shelmerdine says. "I was in the motor home for maybe ten minutes and we were interrupted at least a half dozen times. You gotta sign this. You gotta do that. You gotta be there. That was what his life had become. I'm sure he made time for fishing, but there always was another promotional thing to do."

Shelmerdine was nevertheless caught by Earnhardt's enthusiasm. In the midst of the business, there was still a man who wanted to win the plastic trophy. And this year, Shelmerdine thought, the chances were very good. That record eighth Winston Cup championship was not out of the question.

"This would have been a very good year for Dale," the former crew chief says. "He had a good car and there'd been another change in tires. Goodyear had gone to a hard tire, which made the cars run looser. The tires the last few years, a softer compound . . . anybody could drive fast on those tires. There was such a downforce that you could do anything in the corners. This was different. Experience mattered. Some of those young drivers were going to have problems. This was a situation made for Dale."

There was no proclamation from Earnhardt this year that he was bulletproof, but there didn't have to be. He looked bulletproof. He acted bulletproof. Talking with Darrell Waltrip on Tuesday in an interview for Fox, he couldn't have sounded more contented. He was a happy man.

"How are you doing?" Waltrip asked.

"I'm doing a lot better today than I did several years ago," he said. "Because of family life. I'm a better person than I used to be. Great wife. Great family. I've really got it all right now. Racing. Winning. Competitive. Grandkids. I've got it all, Darrell. I got it all."

"You like Dale Earnhardt?" Waltrip asked.

"I'm pretty happy with him today," Earnhardt said. "He's a pretty straight guy. Stays in line. He gets rambunctious on the racetrack, but that's about it."

The family was fine. The racing was fine. He was the same person on the track, better person in the world. All the ups and all the downs, all the left turns in his life, had brought him to this point. He was settled, confident, happy as he ever had been. He was fierce and mellow, complete, the old man in the young man's game. Still good.

Going through the events of Speed Week—various smaller races leading up to the Daytona 500—he was as competitive as he ever had been. In the Bud Shootout, he was second to Tony Stewart, a nice race, Stewart talking at the end about how nervous he was with Earnhardt in the rearview mirror. The Twin 125 qualifying race was a disappointment, a remarkable string of 10 straight wins halted with an 11th-place finish, but not a large disappointment. That was the race Earnhardt was leading before the freight train of cars came from behind on a late draft and passed him at the end. The beautiful race was the True Value International Race of Champions (IROC) thrill on Friday.

Entering its twenty-fifth year, the IROC annually matched twelve top drivers from the different forms of American racing. They each were put in identically prepared cars, Pontiac Firebirds, then sent onto the track for 40 laps of close combat. Daytona was the first of the four IROC races. Earnhardt was the king of the IROC series.

He had won the event four times, tied with Mark Martin for most wins. In 1999 he won three of the four races to take the title. In 2000, he had taken the title again. His favorite IROC track was Daytona, where had won six of his eleven trophies in the series.

In this year's IROC on the big track, there was no victory but a lot of adventure. On the 26th lap, Earnhardt's green Firebird was sandwiched against the wall by Jeff Burton's purple Firebird. Burton bounced away, colliding with Kenny Brack and Mark Dinsmore, while Earnhardt simply kept moving forward. It was a picture that could have been taken dozens of times in his career.

With two laps to go, he was fighting for the lead with veteran Eddie Cheever of the Indy Racing League. Cheever forced Earnhardt lower, lower, then off the track. Earnhardt somehow missed the retaining wall, came off the grass and back into the race. It was a spectacular racing move, bringing out memories of the Pass In The Grass against Bill Elliott. Earnhardt ultimately finished seventh, Cheever fifth. In the warm-down lap, Earnhardt caught up with Cheever, tapped him on the back, and sent him spinning. Earnhardt then caught up with Cheever on a more personal level, getting out of the car, yelling and screaming, the headlight stare working at full power. Cheever, buckled into the car, could only wonder what would come next.

"Here comes this six-foot guy known as The Intimidator," Cheever said. "I'm thinking I'm not even going to get a punch in. I made a mistake and I apologized."

Earnhardt wound up hugging Cheever. All was forgiven.

"There's all this lore about Earnhardt as a fighter," Ed Hinton points out, "but I have yet to have someone tell me a story about an actual physical confrontation Earnhardt ever had at a track with anyone. That wasn't what he did. He wasn't a brawler. He mostly was a tough guy inside a race car.

"He's been as mad at me as anyone, and he never hit me. In 1989, after the race at Charlotte, he chewed me out. 'Motherfucker' was the nicest thing he called me. This was nose to nose. There were people around who I knew, and they were terrified he was going to kill me. I really wasn't worried. Because that wasn't his style. Now, if A. J. Foyt was mad at you, that was a whole different story."

There was a sweet moment during the week when Earnhardt ran into Kyle Petty. Petty had felt Earnhardt had been avoiding him since the death of Adam and fully understood the reasons. It was all too close, Dale and Dale Jr., Kyle and Adam. Earnhardt apparently had dealt with the feelings, and the two men had a talk. Petty felt good.

There was a moment with Terry Labonte. Earnhardt was on a schedule to break Labonte's Iron Man streak of appearing in 655 straight races—an incredible feat for someone who had been involved in so many crashes—in the fifth race of the season. A promotion was planned to mark the event, Labonte and Earnhardt. Earnhardt mentioned that the promotion would take place if nothing happened to him before the fifth race.

"I think of that statement every day," Labonte later would say.

There were moments everywhere that would become memorable. A smile. A wink. A conversation. These were the snapshots that people didn't even know they were taking, three-by-five glossies that would be framed forever in the mind.

Archie Long, the onetime head of GM Parts, went out on a boat with Earnhardt and Teresa on Thursday night. Archie, retired now, was pretty much going to be a neighbor when Earnhardt's new vacation house was finished in West Palm. Earnhardt's boat wasn't available, so this was a rented boat. Long remembers looking at Earnhardt and marveling.

"What a guy," Long says. "He was confident. He had developed such poise through the years. He was looking forward to Sunday. He said he felt great, as great as he ever had."

———

The minutes before any race are filled with familiar chaos for a driver. He leaves his motor home or the transporter in the garage area or wherever he has been killing time and he walks through an adoring crowd to his car with his wife or friends or maybe some fast-moving television crew.

There is an aura around him, this man in his driving suit and little flame-resistant boots, the daredevil off to be shot out of the cannon or rolled off Niagara Falls in a barrel. He resembles a bullfighter, perhaps, or maybe a boxer. There is a loneliness even as he waves to friends and competitors, signs an autograph for nervous fans. Pared down to essentials, his job is a solitary job. All of the other people, as much as they feel part of the team, part of the scene, will be left in the pits and the stands and the hot-buffet luxury boxes. He, alone, will drive the car.

For Earnhardt, all of this was as natural as going to the store for the morning newspaper. This was what he had done for all of this life, since he sat inside that pink 1976 Ford Club Sedan at that old racetrack in Concord, North Carolina. How many races had he started? How many races in how many places? There were 675 of them in the Winston Cup alone, beginning with that thirsty ride for Ed Negre. Throw in the Busch series, the old Sportsman series, the dirt tracks, the qualifying races, the IROC, all the rest . . . how many? He'd raced four times for money already at Daytona in 2001.

His starting position was seventh, on the inside of the fourth row. Jeff Burton was on the outside. The black car awaited, familiar as family. Earnhardt stopped to talk with different people. He talked with Kyle Petty. He talked with driver Mike Wallace. He talked with Burton, joking about buying a boat.

Stevie Waltrip, Darrell's wife, had taped a card with a Bible verse onto the steering column inside the car. It was a ritual she had started with Neil Bonnett and had continued with Earnhardt. The verse was from Proverbs 18:10: "The name of the Lord is a strong tower; the righteous run into it and are safe."

In the television booth, Waltrip and the Fox crew went on the air, filled with the nervousness and excitement of opening night for a Broadway show. In the press box, the assignments were being handed out by Hinton to the *Orlando Sentinel* reporters covering the race. A twenty-three-year-old sportswriter named Rupen Fofaria, who had never seen a NASCAR race in his life, much less covered one, fresh out of the University of Maryland, wondered what he would be asked to do.

"You cover Dale Earnhardt," Hinton said. "You cover whatever he does. That's your story."

Earnhardt was strapped into the car now, helmet on, all the snaps and buttons of safety already connected. Max Helton held hands with him and with Teresa for the final prayer. Helton says it was a generic prayer, asking for wisdom and safety. Earnhardt kissed Teresa, the sixteen-year-old girl he met at a racetrack, his lifetime partner and confidant and lover and friend.

The engines were started. The radios were checked. Fine.

Forty-three race cars took off for the forty-second running of the Daytona 500, following the pace car, drivers revving the motors, turning the steering wheels back and forth to get the tires warm for more traction. At the far end of the track, the cars disappeared, moving through the first turn.

And Dale Earnhardt was gone.

11

AT THE ALTAR

The ten hawks hovered over the spot where Dale Earnhardt died. This was the next day, the morning. The hawks were thirty feet, maybe forty feet, above the place in the wall of the Daytona Speedway where the No. 3 black Monte Carlo hit.

Nine of the hawks flew mostly in a small circle, around and around. The tenth hawk dove. He would dive to almost the exact spot of the accident, stop, fly back to the circle, then dive again. The same hawk dove every time. Again and again and again.

The two sportswriters saw him.

"I get goose bumps just talking about it," Mike Vega of the Boston Globe *says. "Steve Solloway from the* Portland Press Herald *and I were going back to the track for NASCAR's press conference. We saw this crowd of people, one of those shrines, up by Gate 82. We realized what*

the people were doing because this was the closest place outside to the spot where Earnhardt crashed inside. So we went up there. And then we saw the hawks."

"Hawks," Solloway says. "I don't know the birds of Florida very well. Should there be hawks around the speedway? Is that a normal place for them to be? Seagulls, maybe. There's a million seagulls around Daytona. Hawks? They had those big wingspans. They were beautiful."

"You start thinking," Vega says. "You know, maybe the hawks in the air are the other guys who have died. Neil Bonnett. Adam Petty. All those guys. And the hawk that keeps diving, coming back to the spot, maybe that's . . ."

It all seems strange. Too strange.

"I swear it happened," Solloway says. "We both saw it. Not that we have any idea what it meant. . . ."

Hawks.

THE AFTERMATH

The country singer thought about the conversation. How long ago had it taken place? Had to have been just last week. The week of Daytona. So much had happened. So very much. Dale Earnhardt was on the phone and Kix Brooks was on the road and that was the way it was.

"You should come down to Daytona," Dale said.

"You should come up here and see us," the country singer, one half of the duo Brooks & Dunn, said. "The new CD is out this week. We're kicking off our tour in April."

"I can't get away," Dale said. "You know that."

"I can't get away," the country singer also said. "You know that."

One of them—which one?—then said that time would come, soon enough, when they both would have plenty of opportunities to get together. The other one—which one?—agreed. The race car driver would be too old for racing. The country singer would be off the charts. That was a laugh, but probably the truth. Make the money now because nothing lasts forever. No, it certainly doesn't.

No, not at all.

The church where the country singer sat, Calvary Church in Charlotte, was huge. Giant windows seemed to go to the sky. The floral displays ran across the front of the stage, arrangement after arrangement, one after another, the No. 3 in various red flowers and white flowers, flowers of every color and size and dimension.

Randy Owen, another country singer, the lead voice in the group Alabama, sang a mournful song he had just written called "Goodbye." Sang it nice. A preacher, the Reverend John Cozart of St. Mark's Lutheran Church, Dale's church in Mooresville, read a piece of scripture, Book of John, Chapter 11, the story of Christ bringing Lazarus back from the dead. Another preacher, the Reverend Dale Beaver of Motor Racing Outreach, gave a short sermon. One of the things he told the 3,200 people at the public memorial service, broadcast live on Fox Sports Net, was that they should tell stories. He was sure they already had told stories about Dale and they should tell some more.

The advice seemed sound. Stories? Kix Brooks had stories to tell.

He sat with Teresa and the rest of Dale's family, everybody chewing on his or her own grief. Thirteen busloads of friends and coworkers had come to the service from Dale Earnhardt Incorporated in Mooresville. Fifteen busloads had come from Childress Racing in Welcome. The top NASCAR executives, Mike Helton and William France Jr., the whole France family, was in the church. Famous NASCAR faces were scattered throughout the pews.

The preacher finished and then Randy Owen sang another song, "Angels Among Us," sang it nice, and then Teresa stood up and walked softly in her black dress to the pulpit. A North Carolina state trooper accompanied her. She bent toward the microphone and said the words "Thank you." That's all. The service was finished.

Stories? Yes, the country singer had stories.

———————

"Dale was a complicated guy," Kix Brooks says, "but he definitely had a twelve-year-old's sensibility. . . .

"First time I ever went fishing with him. He catches a five-pound bass. He takes the fish off the hook and just throws it at Hank Jones. Hits him right in the chest. Almost knocks him out of the boat. . . .

"I said to myself, 'You better keep those charming eyes open with this guy.' And that's the way he was. You'd be walking around the pits and all of a sudden you'd be in a headlock. Or against a wall. That was Dale. Saying hello."

Brooks, the shorter half of Brooks & Dunn, the perpetual country duo of the year with eighteen No. 1 songs, met Earnhardt through Jones, the souvenir impresario. Brooks remembers that from the beginning there was an easy feeling with this NASCAR legend. They just connected, clicked, a guy from Shreveport, Louisiana, and a guy from Kannapolis, North Carolina.

Who knows why people become friends, especially later in life? Earnhardt liked country music. Brooks liked stock car racing. They both liked hunting and fishing. They both came from nowhere to somewhere. The easy feeling grew to be an everyday thing.

"We'd call each other two or three times a week, just to talk about nothing," Brooks says. "I'd call him about nothing and he'd call me about nothing. We'd just sit there, talking about nothing.

"He'd always want to know, like, 'What's up with Faith Hill's hair?'

He was a big country fan. I got him a framed dress from Loretta Lynn once, and he was real excited. He loved that. He knew a lot more about country music than I knew about racing. I'd ask him about racing and he'd start to tell me and I'd just get lost. I'd try, but I'd get lost. Finally, he'd say, 'You don't understand any of this, do you?'"

The two men wound up taking vacations together, bringing families along. They wound up hunting and fishing together in all kinds of spots. Earnhardt took Brooks to the reservoir in Kannapolis. No one was allowed to swim or boat or fish in the drinking water. No one except Dale Earnhardt. Throw a line in that water and the bass would fight each other for the hook. Special dispensation: Dale could fish where other people drank.

Brooks & Dunn wound up singing the national anthem at Dale Earnhardt Appreciation Day in Kannapolis on October 5, 1993, standing on the stage with Bonnett and Jeff Gordon and blues singer Delbert McClinton. The mill put out a special black and white commemorative towel and Earnhardt received the key to the city and it was an event. Earnhardt wound up writing the foreword to a book about Brooks & Dunn and appeared in a video for the song "Honky Tonk Truth." That was an experience.

"I got the idea when we went to see him at Indianapolis," Brooks says. "I was walking along pit road and I could see some girls looking at me. They were arguing, 'That's him,' 'No that's not him.' I was feeling pretty good. Then one of them says, 'That's not Dale Earnhardt.'

"The video interchanged shots of him and me. Dale was real nervous about it. He said, 'I don't know how to play the guitar. I don't want to look foolish.' We took him to Las Vegas, where we worked all night on the thing. He was still nervous when it was done, but when it came out he liked it."

There was a fishing trip for marlin off San Salvador in Earnhardt's boat. The day stretched long, no marlin. The big catch was tuna. Tuna and more tuna. Tuna heads, mostly. There were sharks everywhere in the area. Finally, on the way home, Earnhardt spotted two marlin. The men put out their lines. Brooks caught the first marlin of his life. He took out the hook and threw the marlin back into the water to be caught again by someone else.

"Then I went downstairs," he says. "Dale stayed up top, cleaning all the blood and bait off the deck, throwing it into the water. He called me, told me to get up there. He said, 'You've got to see all these sea turtles in the water.' I went up and he just blindsided me, threw me off the boat. Then he drove away, laughing. I'm in the water, in the middle of all this chum, and there's a million sharks in the area.

"Dale had a sense of humor, all right. A dangerous sense of humor, I'd say."

The serious side came out at other times. Brooks remembers Earnhardt being upset all day about forgetting to send a letter to a young boy with cancer. The boy had written the previous week, and Earnhardt had put the letter aside to respond later. When he went to reply, he learned the boy already had died. He kept talking about how bad he felt, how he should have been faster. There would be other conversations, but he always would come back to how bad he felt.

"That was the part of him he didn't let out a lot, but it was there," Brooks says. "I can't even imagine what kinds of letters he must have received every day. He didn't brush 'em off. They meant something to him."

Thinking about the friendship, Brooks says he has decided the similarities between country music and racing were a big part of it. He and Earnhardt were working pretty much to the same crowd, overlapping audiences. The music and the sport always have been tied together, even though NASCAR now often would like to move away from the history toward a wider audience. Marty Robbins, country singer, in fact, was one of the early recognizable driver names in NASCAR. There almost seemed to be an interchangable dream between music and driving, entertaining on Saturday nights for short money, hoping to get ahead, but still happy with what you were doing. Traveling. Having fun. Working with the public, fans.

"I always thought there was a common thread," Brooks says. "He did, too."

Friends. How do you know what makes friends?

It just happens.

———————

The 2001 NASCAR season, in a way, became an extension of the service the country singer, the friend, attended in Charlotte. As the stock car caravan crisscrossed America, sort of like a cat chasing a ball of yarn, every stop became another Sunday-afternoon wake. Rockingham, Vegas, Atlanta, Darlington, Bristol, Fort Worth, Martinsville . . . every track had its moment of silence, its special tribute. Military jet planes flew low, stacked in that missing-man formation. Thousands of fans held their right arms to the sky, three fingers extended, for every third lap. Every track had floral arrangements or the No. 3 painted on the walls or a special prayer or something. Sometimes all of the above.

The man who wasn't there was more important than the men who were there. That was the simple fact.

For a while, it was downright eerie. In the next three races, it was noted that the third lap was run under caution each time. Eerie. The results—Steve Park from DEI winning at Rockingham four days after the memorial service, nemesis Jeff Gordon winning at Vegas, then Kevin Harvick, good God, the replacement in the Goodwrench car, now numbered 29, winning at Atlanta—were eerie.

Rockingham was a story in itself. For starters, Dale Jr. crashed into the wall on the very first lap of the race. The idea that Junior even was in the race, one week after his father's death, walking through all of these sad faces, all of these people wearing his father's hats, No. 3 pennants everywhere, then driving one of those race cars, was remarkable. The idea that he would crash on the first lap, tapped from behind by driver Ron Hornaday, sent on a line into the wall, all so similar to his father's crash, took everyone's breath away. Was he all right? When he climbed out of the car and limped away, the breath came back. Barely.

"The lap belt was a little too tight," he said, oh, man, oh, man. "Just a little bruised up. We'll be OK."

When Park won the race—postponed until Monday when rain arrived following Junior's crash—the emotion kept rolling. Waltrip had won at Daytona, now Park at Rockingham, two-thirds of the DEI team had taken the first two races of the season. Who was writing this stuff?

"I'm glad that it's over," Park said. "It's been an emotional roller coaster this week. I just tried to do everything that Dale Earnhardt taught me to do."

When Harvick won two weeks later at Atlanta . . . the kid wasn't even supposed to be in Winston Cup. He was a Busch series driver, brought in to take Dale's place. He had Dale's crew chief, Kevin Hamlin. He had Dale's pit crew, including big Chocolate Myers. He had Dale's car, the engine, the chassis, the sponsors, the trailer, the PR man, everything the same. He had Dale's life from twenty, almost thirty years ago, the young and fearless man on the move.

"What'd you think?" a reporter asked driver Mark Martin after the race.

"I think Dale would have had a very good car this year," Martin replied.

The NASCAR news off the track also was dominated by Dale. The accident was picked apart on the dissecting table of public opinion. An immediate rip tide of animosity hit Sterling Marlin, whose car bumped the No. 3 out of control, death threats and nastiness, but a larger wave of more rational support, "racin' is racin'," soon replaced it. Junior gave a press conference simply to show his support for the beleaguered Marlin. That helped a lot.

Two controversies evolved. The first concerned Earnhardt's seat belt. Did it break? Was it cut? Did it stay together? The second concerned the autopsy photos of Earnhardt. Should they be made public?

The *Orlando Sentinel* was in the front of both battles. NASCAR first claimed that Earnhardt died because his seat belt broke. The *Sentinel* challenged that contention, requesting that an independent expert be allowed to view the autopsy report. A deal was made before a Florida judge to allow one expert, Dr. Barry Meyers of Duke University, to see the photos. When Dr. Meyers said that the cause of death was not related to a possible broken seat belt but a basal skull fracture from the force of the collision, same as the other three deaths a year ago, NASCAR stepped back from its earlier pronouncement, but said it was going to have its own experts make a judgment.

The *Sentinel* found an emergency worker from the accident scene who said the seat belt had been intact when he reached Earnhardt. NASCAR produced a picture from the Daytona police department showing a frayed and severed seat belt. Back and forth. Nobody looked very good in the arguments except for Teresa Earnhardt, who testified in court, dignified and calm, that she did not want the autopsy photos released because she did not want them to appear in supermarket tabloids and on the Internet. That made sense.

Junior slowly returned in front of the cameras. His sister, Kelley, once said she worried about him in high school because he was so slender, so shy. The life of the NASCAR hero becomes snack food for public consumption. His family becomes part of the package. The people who love the hero want to know all they can about him to feed their love. The people who hate the hero want to know so they can feed their hate. The children of the heroes have to deal with all this daily. Kelley always worried about the effect of it all on her brother.

Now, the intensity magnified a hundred fold, strangers looking at him with tears in their eyes, the son seemed to be holding up quite well. He said his life had changed in a moment. He was much more religious now, much more responsible. He was an adult. His first public interview was with Pat Robertson on *The 700 Club,* the Christian broadcasting show. His second interview was with Darrell Waltrip on Fox.

"I know I was surprised by the outpouring of emotion from the fans, not just in our community but all over the world, that came in response to your father's death," Waltrip said at one point. "Did you have any idea?"

"I think it surprised everybody," Junior replied. "It surprised me quite a bit. You realize exactly how many people are paying attention. There are more people watching and listening than you think. And then there are those who never sat down to watch a race before, but then they hear John down the street talking about it and they see how their friend Bill reacted and must have said to themselves, 'Man, this guy meant a lot to a lot of people. Tell me a bit about this guy.' It makes me feel good to see what he meant to so many people."

And that was the enduring story of the spring and then through the summer and into the fall, how much Dale Earnhardt had meant to so many people, how much he had mattered. The crowds kept coming, week after week, dressed in their black hats and their No. 3 T-shirts, everyone a little lost, everyone putting one foot after the next, moving forward. The man who wasn't there was the one who mattered most in the 2001 NASCAR season.

That was simple fact.

The country singer wasn't going to do a tribute to his friend. He looked around the landscape and didn't like what was happening to the memory of Dale Earnhardt. He saw too many fast-buck schemes. He saw too many people talking as if they had known the man, were close as brothers, "when they didn't know him from Adam." He didn't want to be a part of that.

"The reporters, in fact, came to my house after he died," Kix Brooks says. "I wouldn't talk to them. Our friendship was private. I didn't want to do anything that would change that."

As the days passed, his mind slowly changed. There was a Brooks & Dunn song, "You're Gonna Miss Me When I'm Gone" that Earnhardt always liked from the 1994 album *Waitin' on Sundown*. He said it reminded him of Neil Bonnett every time he heard it. The song now reminded Brooks of Dale Earnhardt.

You better kiss me
'Cause you're gonna miss me
When I'm gone . . .

The country singer began doing a talking part in the middle of the song about his friend. He decided that a tribute was a tribute. He wasn't taking advantage of anything, anyone. He was paying homage to someone who meant a lot not only to him, but to a lot of other people.

"The fans out there really appreciated that song," Brooks says in the middle of Brooks & Dunn's Neon Circus & Wild West Show tour. "We do it every night. There's a lot of people out there who are really lost without him. He was a very real individual. As hard-core and as rednecked as you could get, but just real."

A number of analogies have been used, since his death, to describe this man who rode around and around the racetracks of America. Cowboy analogies have been very big. John Wayne has been mentioned a lot. Kyle Petty once went through the list of NASCAR drivers and compared each of them to an animal. He said Dale Earnhardt would have been a grizzly bear. Not a stuffed grizzly bear, a live one, coming out of the forest.

The country singer and good friend is asked who Earnhardt would resemble most in country music. George Jones?

"Nah," Kix Brooks says after a moment's thought. "I would say, more like Merle Haggard."

Perfect.

EPILOGUE

The old men start arriving around 6:30 in the morning at Rodney Huffman's Citgo station on Jackson Park Road in Kannapolis and stay till just about noon. There is no roll call, no attendance chart kept, but in a normal week the same cast of a dozen or more characters will appear, one morning or another, nothing to do, killing time for another soft day at the end of a lifetime of harder ones. The Liars Club—there's the sign, "Liars Club," on the yellowed wall, over near the coffeepot, 25 cents a cup—has a fluid membership.

Richard Anderson, the sixty-five-year-old former mayor of Kannapolis, tends the pumps, going outside when a car rolls over the air hose and rings the bell. Bing. Sometimes Claude Elwood does the job. He's about a hundred years old now, Claude, just back from his fifth coronary bypass surgery. Bing. He has been here thirty years, pumping gas. Maybe forty.

The other old guys mostly just talk. They sit outside in the summer. Wives are dead. Children are gone. The time is 10 A.M. right now. Two hours to go until lunch. Seven liars are here at the moment.

"Remember that fellow who had the garbage business?" Harry Overcash says. "Maybe twenty-five, thirty years ago? He picked up the garbage here. A little guy, slender. A black guy. Brought the garbage back home to his pig farm? To feed the pigs?"

"Don't believe I do," Grant Lawson says.

"One day he brings the garbage back and he drops dead on the floor of the barn with a heart attack! Remember what happened?"

"Tell me again."

"The pigs ate him!"

"Oh, yeah. I remember now."

"Left nothing but bones!"

"Oh, yeah."

(Pause.)

"I saw a thing on television the other night," Grant Lawson says. "Anybody else see it? There was a report about feces in hamburger. Made you sick."

The rhythms do not change at Rodney Huffman's Citgo. The bizarre and the mundane are all open to discussion. World War II and Korea seem to have finished just about last Thursday. Women are still pretty. Kids are crazy. The mills have been mismanaged into the state they're in. The local government is terrible. The world has gone to hell. The usual stuff.

Dale.

———

"He's buried back on his property, back in the woods," Richard Anderson says. "It's all supposed to be a big secret, but that's where he is. They're building a mausoleum. But the public never will see it."

"It's all hush-hush," Grant Lawson says. "The workers are all told to keep quiet. I think they have to sign something."

"They brought him in in a white hearse," Harry Overcash says. "That's what I heard. A white hearse!"

Dale is a subject of constant conversation.

There has never been anyone else like Dale Earnhardt to come from Kannapolis. That is pretty much agreed. He put Kannapolis on the map! Think of Kannapolis and you think of Dale Earnhardt. Not even the mills, back when they were going good, did what Dale did. He went out into the great beyond and knocked 'em dead. He knew singers and movie stars. He knew the President. Didn't George W., himself, say hello to Teresa and the kids when he stopped in Charlotte not too long ago? The President. Dale Earnhardt was big.

"What's happened at the baseball stadium?" someone asks. "Did they still put in that private box that Dale was going to have? The one with the easy chair and the phone?"

"Dale bought the local baseball team last year," Richard Anderson explains. "There was a big press conference. It's a minor-league team. Class A. Dale and Bruton Smith, the owner of the track in Concord, and Rick Hendrick, the car owner, all put up money. They renamed the team the Kannapolis Intimidators. They used to be the Piedmont Boll Weevils. Didn't draw much. They were hoping Dale being involved would get people out there to see him. Probably would have happened, too, but not now."

"Nobody goes there now," someone says.

"The players are all from South America or somewhere," someone else says. "Rookies. You just don't know who they are."

"What about the private box?" Harry Overcash asks. "I can understand Dale would have needed that box—he'd always be busy, having to call Hong Kong or Los Angeles or someplace. Does anyone else use it?"

Nobody knows.

The beauty of having a local guy become famous is that the experience is shared. Everybody gets to take the ride with him in even the slightest way. There is a connection, a touch, no matter how small. See that supermarket? That's where he bought his groceries. See that stoplight? Saw him there once. He was wearing those sunglasses. Stared at me. There always is a friend or a second cousin who went to the same church or whose kids went to the same school as the famous man's children. There always is something.

Richard Anderson says he still wants to pay his respects to Martha, Dale's mother. He knows Martha. He didn't know Dale, not really, but he knows Martha. There was no point going to her house, with all the other people visiting, the crowd, but now it would seem to be the proper time. Time to talk. Martha's a fine lady. Danny and Randy, Dale's brothers, are fine people, too. Dale was good people. Busy all the time, but good people.

Ask Rodney.

Dale bought Rodney's house. Rodney, tell 'em . . .

"He called me up and said, 'Huffman, it's Earnhardt,' just like that," Rodney Huffman, a younger man, the owner of the service station, says as he takes a break from working on the innards of some little Japanese engine that looks like a sewing machine. "I owned a piece of property that was next to his. He wanted to buy it, wanted to have his brother live in the house. We had some discussions and finally I sold it. Gave me the money to live where I live now. A better house."

There was a visit, Rodney says, before Dale bought the property. Dale wanted to drive around and check out the land. He showed up in a big black truck. He asked Rodney to join him.

"You don't mind driving with an old stock car racer, do you?" Earnhardt asked.

Rodney was nervous. They bumped and thumped around the land. Rodney pointed out various features. Earnhardt nodded. He didn't drive crazy or anything. Normal. Until he jammed on the brakes. Rodney hit his head. Something had run across the path.

"What's that?" Earnhardt said.

"Probably a beaver," Rodney replied. "There's a stream right near where we are and a bunch of beavers live there."

Earnhardt reached under his seat and pulled out a long pistol. Rodney thinks it was a .44.

"Would it be OK if we shot it?" Earnhardt asked.

Rodney smiles.

"I told him," Rodney says, "if you buy the property, you can shoot any damn thing you want.'"

The official stop for the followers of Dale to pay their respects is his corporate headquarters ten miles away on Coddle Creek Road in

Mooresville. Tour buses arrive daily. Even more people arrive in twos and threes, kids falling out of the backseat of family cars, everybody wearing some kind of No. 3 merchandise.

It is an ugly building, Dale Earnhardt Incorporated, big and new and showy, a poor man's idea of a rich man's luxury. The sides are covered in mirror glass and gold, a big and ornate entrance in the front. The building sticks out of the landscape at the edge of Earnhardt's property like some Las Vegas bad dream. The parts that are open to the public, the museum and gift shop, are curiously sterile and formal. Dull.

The guestbook has a sign above it that requests visitors to sign only their name and address, no personal messages. The floors are polished. The air is climate controlled. There is a hush instead of noise.

Gone are all remnants of the unfinished man who roared onto the scene, brash and countrified and fearless. The cars and the trophies in the museum are waxed and shined showpieces. A sequence of pictures on one wall, written explanations below, shows how the furniture for the upstairs boardroom and offices was hand-carved in Europe, how the chefs prepare elegant meals in the stainless-steel kitchen. The big display is a six-foot-tall head shot of Dale, set in the middle of a room full of automobiles and flowers, the picture hung under a skylight. The shadows on his smiling face change with the movement of the sun. This is a recent picture, to be sure. He is wearing a tuxedo.

"Where are the pictures of him with his family?" a psychologist, a visitor from Providence, Rhode Island, says. "Where's the picture of the house where he grew up? His brothers and sisters? Where are the pictures from the races he didn't win? Where is all the stuff from when he was getting started? This is a monument to his success, maybe, all the stuff he collected, but it doesn't tell us how he got there."

The truth of the man is somewhere else.

Why did so many people let him get so close to their hearts? Why were they so upset when he died? There was grease underneath the fingernails of the character who brought out all this love. There was that defiance in his eyes. If he were some hard-driving Elvis—another analogy used often—he was the Elvis on *The Ed Sullivan Show,* the soulful renegade, an explosion best captured with no camera angles below the waist lest the children be watching and anybody be offended. He was raw and dirty and great. He was one of us, but turned out better. He was human.

He went where we were afraid to go. . . .

He did what we were afraid to do. . . .

He roared.

───────

"He was better than any of them," someone says at Rodney Huffman's Citgo. "His daddy was good, but Dale was better. He was better than Richard Petty or David Pearson. He was better even than Curtis Turner."

"Curtis Turner was something on the dirt," someone else says. "He'd start putting his car into a slide halfway down the straightaway. Never seen anything like it. He'd drive half the race looking in toward the infield."

"Dale Earnhardt was better than Curtis Turner. Dale Earnhardt was the best."

Maybe he was local for everybody. Maybe that was it. Maybe television brought him into the home and made him everybody's brash next-door neighbor. Maybe he was that crazy kid in everybody's neighborhood, the one who does the damnedest things, drives you to distraction in the beginning, but makes you smile in the end when he becomes a huge success. What a story. Maybe everywhere was Kannapolis. Maybe Dale Earnhardt was everybody's local boy makes good.

Maybe half the country sits inside Rodney's garage. Maybe so.

"I give him a lot of respect," Claude Elwood, a hundred years old and five bypasses, says. "That racing's awful hard. . . ."

(Pause.)

"Tried it one time, myself. . . ."

(Pause.)

"Only lasted three or four laps. . . ."

(Pause.)

"Always was turning that wheel. You'd just get done with the first turn and there it was, you'd be starting into that second turn. . . ."

(Pause.)

(Pause.)

"Them turns come awful fast."

BIBLIOGRAPHY

The basic facts of Dale Earnhardt's life have been laid out in many places. A flurry of tribute magazines appeared after the events of February 18, 2001, and many newspapers have covered the public moments of this private man. These publications were all sources, as were the following books:

Reporters of the *Charlotte Observer. Dale Earnhardt: Rear View Mirror.* Champaign, IL. Sports Publishing, Inc. Rev. 2001.

Moriarty, Frank. *Dale Earnhardt.* New York, MetroBooks. 2001.

Phillips, Benny, and Ben Blake with Dale Earnhardt. *Dale Earnhardt—Determined.* Charlotte, NC. UMI Publications. 1998.

Regruth, John. *Dale Earnhardt: The Final Record.* Osceola, WI. MBI Publishing. 2001.

Uehorn, Frank. *The Intimidator.* Asheboro, NC. Down Home Press. Rev. 1999.

Wilkinson, Sylvia. *Dirt Tracks to Glory.* Chapel Hill, NC. Algonquin Books. 1983.

© MARY ELLEN FORGETTE

ABOUT THE AUTHOR

A senior writer for S*ports Illustrated,* Leigh Montville also served for twenty-one years as a sports columnist for the *Boston Globe.* His previous books include *Manute: The Center of Two Worlds* and, with Jim Calhoun, *Dare to Dream* (Broadway Books, 1999). Montville lives in Winthrop, Massachusetts.